WILL GOD

SET UP A

VISIBLE KINGDOM

ON EARTH?

by

Henry Clay Morrison

First Fruits Press
Wilmore, Kentucky
c2012

ISBN: 9781621710394

Will God set up a Visible Kingdom on Earth? by H.C. Morrison.
First Fruits Press, © 2012
Originally published by the Pentecostal Publishing Company, ©1934

Digital version at http://place.asburyseminary.edu/firstfruitsheritagematerial/21

First Fruits Press is a digital imprint of the Asbury Theological Seminary, B.L. Fisher Library. Asbury Theological Seminary is the legal owner of the material previously published by the Pentecostal Publishing Co. and reserves the right to release new editions of this material as well as new material produced by Asbury Theological Seminary. Its publications are available for noncommercial and educational uses, such as research, teaching and private study. First Fruits Press has licensed the digital version of this work under the Creative Commons Attribution Noncommercial 3.0 United States License. To view a copy of this license, visit http://creativecommons.org/licenses/by-nc/3.0/us/.

For all other uses, contact:

First Fruits Press
B.L. Fisher Library
Asbury Theological Seminary
204 N. Lexington Ave.
Wilmore, KY 40390
http://place.asburyseminary.edu/firstfruits

Morrison, H. C. (Henry Clay), 1857-1942
  Will God set up a visible kingdom on Earth? / by H.C. Morrison.
Wilmore, Ky. : First Fruits Press, c2012.
158 p. ; 21 cm.
Reprint. Previously published: Louisville, Ky. : Pentecostal Publishing Company, c1934.
ISBN: 9781621710394 (pbk.)
  1. Millennium. 2. Second Advent. 3. Millennium (Eschatology). I. Title.
BT890 .M77 2012

Cover design by Jane Brannen

asburyseminary.edu
800.2ASBURY
204 North Lexington Avenue
Wilmore, Kentucky 40390

WILL GOD
Set up a Visible Kingdom
ON EARTH?

By

Rev. H. C. Morrison, D. D.

Author of

"The Christ of The Gospels," "Remarkable Conversions," "The Two Lawyers," "Sermons for the Times," "Lectures on Prophecy," "Optimism of Premillennialism," "Is the World Growing Better; or, Is the World Growing Worse."

First Edition, April 1st
Second Edition, April 15th
Third Edition, April 24th
Fourth Edition, May 1st
Fifth Edition, May 20th

PENTECOSTAL PUBLISHING COMPANY,
LOUISVILLE, KENTUCKY.

COPYRIGHT, 1934, BY
PENTECOSTAL PUBLISHING COMPANY,
LOUISVILLE, KENTUCKY

Dedicated to the Faithful People who have furnished the means to build and support Asbury College.

I am grateful to my Wife, who has entered very fully with me into the spirit and purpose of this book, and has rendered great assistance in preparing it for the press.

My thanks are due Miss Helen Bishop, of Wilmore, Ky., who typed a number of chapters in this volume.

This book is written, published and sent out with a double purpose. We wish to provoke thought and the reading of the Scriptures on the subject of the Appearing and Reign of our Lord Jesus Christ. We desire through its publication and sale, to render financial aid in this time of stress, to Asbury College. Fifty cents of the sale of each copy will go into a fund for the assistance of this institution which has rendered such gracious service to a multitude of splendid young Christian people who are successful soul winners in the wide harvest field of Christian evangelism. We solicit the sympathy and assistance of the Lord's people, everywhere.

Faithfully yours,
H. C. MORRISON.

PREFACE

The fulfillment of Prophecy is one of the most powerful proofs of the existence of God, His knowledge of future events and His power to communicate His knowledge to men, and so inspire them that they can look deep into the future and tell with remarkable accuracy of events that will take place thousands of years from the time of their predictions.

The Bible contains many such prophecies which have been uttered by men who claimed to be taught of God, and have been fulfilled with such detail that there is no way to explain them, except that there is a God, and that He can, and does, communicate a knowledge of future events to men.

In this book we have gone to prophetic portions of the Holy Scriptures for the proof of the events of which we have written. The Coming and Reign of the Lord Jesus Christ are so clearly taught by the prophets, so much of what they foretold has come to pass, as they predicted, that it is quite reasonable to believe that their prophecies which have not yet been fulfilled will, in due time, be enacted into history.

It is very evident to thoughtful people of all creeds and classes, that human history is on the eve of some great and radical changes. Things cannot remain long, as they now are. We are approaching a titanic struggle between Capital and Labor. If time lasts for any number of years, before the appearing of our Lord, there is bound to be a new economic and social order. What has happened in Russia, and what is transpiring in Germany, does not promise that the impending change will bring larger freedom and greater happiness to the people.

It may be we are approaching the coming of Christ, and the setting up of a Divine Order in the world. God has broken human history up into dispensations, or ages. It appears that, when an age has served its purpose, it comes to a close and God introduces a new and better age.

After the Flood, God having saved what good people there were, brought them over into a new and better age. The Hebrew age was far superior to the Antediluvian age. At its close, God brought in the Gentile or Church age, which has been a vast improvement on the Hebrew age. It may be that He is now about to bring in the Kingdom age under the reign of Christ.

There is one thing which is quite manifest: The people have lost confidence in man's ability to bring in a warless age of justice and peace. They are longing for some one they can trust; some one who will bring justice and peace among men and nations. Personally, I cannot believe any sort of socialism or communism, with its free love and blasphemy, can bring anything but worse confusion to the state, and deeper degradation to the individual.

Nothing but the Coming of Christ into the world will bring order out of its confusion, peace out of its war, and a proper adjustment of human relationships. The Second Coming of Christ will not be for the final judgment, but a thousand years of righteous government among men. After this, Satan is to be loosed for a little season and then the last tragic acts of human history, and the final judgment.

The Scriptures plainly teach that, as we approach the end of this age, there will be a riot of sin, wickedness, war and bloodshed, with the fearful judgments of God visited upon a rebellious and blasphemous world. Many devout and thoughtful people believe that the trend and drift of the present time is toward the fulfillment of prophecies in Daniel, and the book of Revelation, of lawlessness, blasphemy, the persecution of the righteous, the appearing of the Man of sin, the last war of blood and fire, culminating in the battle of Armageddon, and the Coming of the Lord.

At the time of the Flood the righteous were saved in the Ark. At the fall and destruction of Palestine and Jerusalem, the disciples of Christ fled to the mountains and were saved. In the final tribulation there is a gracious promise of the saints being caught up to safety. Blessed are they who are not entangled with the things of the world when that auspicious hour shall come. Let us labor as if the Master delayed His coming. Let us watch with lamps trimmed and burning as if He should appear at this midnight, or in the morning.

If the readers of this book expect me in any sort of dogmatic manner to try to fix dates, or go into details, with reference to the time of Christ's coming, and the manner of His government of the world, they will be disappointed. That He will come, that His reign upon the earth will bring in a period of justice and peace among men and nations, is clearly taught in the Scriptures.

There are wide ranges for thought and interesting speculation about what shall take place during that golden age of peace and good will among men.

H. C. MORRISON.

CONTENTS

CHAPTERS

1. God's Covenant with Abraham... 15
2. The Jews in Prophecy 23
3. The Dispersion of the Jews...... 31
4. The Restoration of the Jews..... 41
5. Will God Set Up a Visible Kingdom on Earth? 69
6. Who Will Be the King? 79
7. Jesus Christ is Coming Back to This Earth. 89
8. What Sort of Rulership Will Christ Give the World? 97
9. When Will Jesus Come?........ 105
10. The Signs of the Coming of the Lord. 119
11. The Failure of Human Governments. 133
12. The Man of Sin; or, The End of The Age 143

CHAPTER I.

GOD'S COVENANT WITH ABRAHAM.

The promises of God to Abraham were also for his descendants, the Israelites, embracing all of the Hebrews, both Israel and Judah. Not only would God bless Abraham and his seed, but through them all the nations of the earth. We read: "Now the Lord had said unto Abraham, Get thee out of thy country, and from thy kindred, and from thy father's house, unto a land that I will show thee: And I will make of thee a great nation, and I will bless thee and make thy name great; and thou shalt be a blessing: And I will bless them that bless thee, and curse him that curseth thee: and in thee shall all families of the earth be blessed." Gen. 12:1-3.

It is worthy of notice that God says, "I will curse him that curseth thee." Here is a promise that those who punish Israel will be punished. History affords a fulfillment of this warning which God gives to all nations. Those nations that have indulged in severe and unreasonable treatment of the Jewish people have certainly been punished. Reading on, we find a number of gracious promises to Abraham: "And I will make thee exceeding fruitful, and I will make nations of thee, and kings shall come out of thee. And I will establish my covenant between me and thee and thy seed after thee in their generations for an everlasting covenant, to be a God unto thee, and to thy seed after thee." Gen. 17:6, 7. Reading further we find this promise: "And I will take you to me for a people, and I will be to you a God: and ye shall know that I am the Lord your God, which bringeth you out from under the burdens of the Egyptians." Ex. 6:7. Further on, we read: "Now therefore, if ye will obey my voice indeed, and keep my covenant, then ye shall be a peculiar treasure unto me above all people: for all the earth is mine: And ye shall be unto me a kingdom of priests, and an holy nation.

VISIBLE KINGDOM ON EARTH 17

These are the words thou shalt speak unto the children of Israel." Ex. 19:5, 6.

Speaking of the Israelites, Moses says, "The Lord shall establish thee an holy people unto himself, as he hath sworn unto thee, if thou shalt keep the commandments of the Lord thy God, and walk in his ways. And all people of the earth shall see that thou art called by the name of the Lord; and they shall be afraid of thee." Deut. 28:9, 10.

This same covenant of special blessing to Israel was continued long after the death of Abraham and Moses, and the establishing of Israel in the land of Canaan. We read: "Be ye mindful always of his covenant; the word which he commanded to a thousand generations; Even of the covenant which he made with Abraham, and of his oath unto Isaac; And hath confirmed the same to Jacob for a law, and to Israel for an everlasting covenant. 1 Chron. 16: 15-17.

The reader will notice at once that the promises of God to Israel and His covenant with them were to be binding and in force forever. We read in Jeremiah 11:2-5: "Hear ye the words of this covenant, and speak unto the men of Judah, and to the inhabitants of Jerusalem; And say unto them, Thus saith the Lord God of Israel; Cursed be the man that obeyeth not the words of this covenant, Which I commanded your fathers in the day that I brought them forth out of the land of Egypt, from the iron furnace, saying, Obey my voice, and do them, according to all which I command you: so shall ye be my people, and I will be your God. That I may perform the oath which I have sworn unto your fathers, to give them a land flowing with milk and honey, as it is this day. Then answered I, and said, So be it, O Lord."

As we go forward searching the Scriptures, we find this divine covenant which God entered into with Abraham and his

VISIBLE KINGDOM ON EARTH

seed, in the prophets, in the Psalms, and in the Gospels, showing that it was clearly understood that Israel was God's chosen people, that His covenant was constantly renewed and abiding, taught and impressed upon His chosen people, always conditioned upon their obedience to His commandments and the careful observance of His laws.

King David's last charge and exhortation to Israel was most impressive. It reads: "Now therefore in the sight of all Israel the congregation of the Lord, and in the audience of our God, keep and seek for all the commandments of the Lord your God: that ye may possess this good land, and leave it for an inheritance for your children after you for ever." 1 Chron. 28:8.

No king or statesman ever packed more wisdom into a few words than these last charges of David to Israel. Israel failed to keep her covenant with God. She broke her vows, trampled upon divine law, and soon her hills were covered with the tents of her pagan foes, her valleys trembled under the charge of the chariots of her victorious enemies and her people were led away in chains of captivity. Had Israel kept the covenant of the Lord, walked in harmony with His laws, in time, the pagan peoples in the various nations surrounding Israel would have been illuminated with divine truth and would have come to Jerusalem to see the glory of the temple, to listen to the teachings of the priests, and would have carried back to their peoples the knowledge of the true God. By and by they would have cast aside their idols and gradually have come to worship the true and only God. Had this occurred, the history of the world would have been far different and a vast improvement on what it is.

Israel backslid, departed from God, worshipped the idols of her pagan neighbors and, in the end, the peoples whom they should have evangelized and saved, conquered them, burned their temple, destroyed the holy city, and enslaved them. Nevertheless we find in prophecy gracious promises for the restoration of Israel, which, it appears, are now beginning to be fulfilled. St. Paul utters a prophecy full of promise for the final salvation and restoration of God's chosen people who, from the first, were designed to perform a most important part in the great drama of human history and in the salvation of mankind. We read: "Behold therefore the goodness and severity of God: on them which fell, severity; but toward thee, goodness, if thou continue in his goodness; otherwise thou also shalt be cut off. And they also, if they abide not still in unbelief, shall be graffed in: for God is able to graff them in again. For if thou wert cut out of the olive tree which is wild by nature, and wert graffed contrary to nature into a good olive tree; how much more shall these, which be the natural branches, be graffed into their own olive tree? For I would not, brethren, that ye should be ignorant of this mystery, lest ye should be wise in your own conceits; that blindness in part is happened to Israel, until the fulness of the Gentiles be come in. And so all Israel shall be saved: as it is written, There shall come out of Sion the Deliverer, and shall turn away ungodliness from Jacob: For this is my covenant unto them, when I shall take away their sins." Romans 11:22-27.

We find in this exhortation of the great apostle a warning to the Gentiles and a promise to Israel. World events are in perfect harmony with prophecy concerning the persecution of the Jews and their final restoration to Palestine. It is very evident that the Jews are yet to play a very important part in world affairs and the bringing in of the Kingdom of God on earth.

CHAPTER II.
THE JEWS IN PROPHECY.

I have read somewhere that Emperor Wilhelm of Germany, grandfather of the deposed Kaiser, during one of his campaigns, sitting with his staff around a campfire at night, said to his chaplain, "Chaplain, give me in a word the best external evidence of the divine inspiration of the Bible. I do not wish a discussion or an argument, but a concrete statement." It is said that the chaplain saluted, and answered, "Sire, the Jews!" "Ha!" said the Emperor, "That is correct. The Jews, as we have them in prophecy, in history, and in the world today, are a powerful external proof of the divine inspiration of the Holy Scriptures."

I do not know that this conversation took place. I know it could have occurred and have been quite correct, both as to the statement of the chaplain and the comment of the Emperor. The ancient prophets of

Israel blazed a trail through the future, which has become the highway of history; the march of human events has been in such remarkable harmony with the foretelling of the Hebrew seers that one is compelled to believe that they were divinely inspired. The fulfillment of prophetic prediction reaching out centuries, even thousands of years, beyond the times in which the prophets lived and spoke, is one of the most powerful proofs that there is a God, that He knows all things and that He has inspired men with a knowledge which enabled them to look far into the future and tell of coming events with wonderful accuracy.

As a very small boy during the Civil War, I often sat on the fence at the roadside and watched the soldiers marching by. There were certain regiments of infantry, batteries of artillery, and divisions of cavalry that had made themselves famous by some splendid deed of valor that had turned

VISIBLE KINGDM ON EARTH 25

the tide of battle and brought victory when defeat seemed almost certain. I was eager to see these distinguished troops and would ask of some passing soldier, "What regiment, what battery, or what cavalry is this now passing?" I felt a special interest in those men who had performed dangerous and heroic deeds. I was anxious to know just who and what was passing by.

I am a bit that way with reference to the prophecies contained in the Holy Scriptures. I would like to know, if possible, just what prophetic predictions are being enacted into history. I should like to know where we are, and who, and what, is on the stage at the present time. God set the cogs in the wheel of prophecy so that they would fit with such accuracy into the cogs on the wheel of history that we could have solid ground on which to stand and believe that the holy prophets were inspired by the Holy Spirit.

The ancient prophets in their predictions of the coming doom of the great cities of Babylon, Nineveh, Tyre, and Jerusalem, were not only the objects of ridicule, but of most cruel persecution, often tortured to death. To all human appearance, those prophets were bound to be mistaken when they foretold the utter destruction of the cities which, at the time of their speaking, seemed impregnable. They were so vast, so well built, such marts of trade, such centers of wealth and culture, political influence and power; they were surrounded by walls so thick and high, and so carefully guarded, that it seemed quite childish that long-bearded, serious, poorly-clad old men should be going about telling the people that these triumphs of human wisdom and skill, the products of centuries of toil and achievement, would become heaps of ruin and desolation, the abiding place of serpents, wild beasts, and the hooting of doleful owls. However, the words of the ridiculed and hated dreamers have come true. Long ago the wheels of time rolled through the dust and ashes of all that remained where those proud cities stood in seeming indestructible endurance. Today archæologists must search and dig with more or less difficulty in locating the centers and boundaries of those vast cities of a proud, godless and decayed pagan civilization.

The prophetic method which God has used in building up much of the Holy Scriptures makes it impossible for the Bible to grow old, or obsolete. It marches ahead of history. It constantly beckons us on with a divine light, looking into the unfolding future. It gives us certain data for the understanding of conditions about us, along with the past and the future, which cannot be found outside of the Holy Scriptures. No devout person can read prophecy with even a partial acquaintance with what has gone before, is now being enacted upon the stage of the present, and what the lifting curtains of the future will reveal, without being profoundly impressed that the Bible is a divinely-inspired book, that the men who saw so deeply into the future and foretold coming events with such accurate detail, cannot be accounted for apart from the fact that they were taught of God, that they had a divine knowledge communicated to them by the Holy Spirit.

The writings of Isaiah, Jeremiah, and Ezekiel are largely made up of exhortations, warnings, and foretellings to Israel of their coming captivity and dispersion among the nations, with the sufferings and sorrows which would come to them because of their sins. These prophecies also contain gracious promises of final restoration to their fatherland. Christ appears all through these prophecies with gracious hope of their final salvation, and His peaceful and glorious reign over God's chosen people, as well as the Gentile world.

It appears that present day statesmen, writers and the rulers and leaders of the

VISIBLE KINGDOM ON EARTH

people act as if the prophetic portions of the Bible did not exist. Many ministers of the gospel, especially those who are under the spell of Modern Liberalism, are found not only to pay no heed to the prophecies of the Hebrew seers except they insist that they knew nothing of the future, and this, while so much of prophecy has been fulfilled and is being fulfilled before our eyes. Those who read prophecy, and believe that these men were divinely inspired, are not at all surprised at the offering of Palestine to returning Jews as one of the results of the World War.

God has spoken through holy men. His word cannot fail. As events in the great plan of the ages move forward prophecy becomes history.

CHAPTER III.
THE DISPERSION OF THE JEWS.

Reading the prophets we shall find that these holy men were constantly rebuking their people for their idolatry and wickedness, exhorting them to repentance and warning them of the judgments of God, and the fact that, in punishing them, they would eventually be carried captive into foreign countries, and predicting the very persecutions and sorrows to which they have been subjected through the centuries.

We are especially impressed with one of these warnings found in Deuteronomy 28:37: "And thou shalt become an astonishment, a proverb, and a byword among all nations whither the Lord shall lead thee." This prophecy has been fulfilled in a most remarkable way. How common the saying, "He is nothing but a Jew," "he is as dishonest as a Jew," "he is no more trustworthy than a Jew," "he is a wandering Jew." We give here a rather lengthy quotation from the fourth chapter of Deuteronomy of a warning to Israel uttered by Moses before his departure from them:

"Take heed unto yourselves, lest ye forget the covenant of the Lord your God, which he made with you, and make you a graven image, or the likeness of anything which the Lord thy God hath forbidden thee. For the Lord thy God is a consuming fire, even a jealous God. When thou shalt beget children, and children's children, and ye shall have remained long in the land, and shall corrupt yourselves, and make a graven image, or the likeness of anything, and shall do evil in the sight of the Lord thy God, to provoke him to anger; I call heaven and earth to witness against you this day, that ye shall soon utterly perish from off the land whereunto ye go over Jordan to possess it; ye shall not prolong your days upon it, but shall utterly be destroyed. And the Lord shall scatter you among the nations, and ye shall be left few in number among

VISIBLE KINGDOM ON EARTH 33

the heathen, whither the Lord shall lead you." Deut. 4:23-27.

It would take many chapters of a book of this kind to contain the prophecies both by the major and minor prophets concerning the dispersion of Israel among the nations. We read from Amos, "For, lo, I will command, and I will sift the house of Israel among all nations, like as corn is sifted in a sieve, yet shall not the least grain fall upon the earth. All the sinners of my people shall die by the sword, which say, the evil shall not overtake nor prevent us." Amos 9:10. Amos is assuring them that their conceit cannot protect them although they flatter themselves that they shall escape. The truth is that the Jews have been tortured, oppressed, robbed, and butchered in many nations throughout the centuries. King David prophesies, looking into the future, of the sins and retributions that shall come upon the people; "Thou hast given us like sheep appointed for meat; and hast scattered us among the heathen. Thou sellest thy people for nought, and dost not increase thy wealth by their price. Thou makest us a reproach to our neighbors, a scorn and a derision to them that are round about us." Psalm 44:11-13.

This prophecy of the Psalmist has not only been fulfilled among heathen countries but in most of the civilized nations. It is being fulfilled at the present time in Germany. The Jews have suffered fearfully there, being put out of office and so hampered in their business enterprises that many of them are practically bankrupt. The opposition to Jews in Germany has been of a character that many of them who could do so have fled from the country. The prophets spoke as they were moved by the Holy Spirit and the Holy Spirit knew what would come to pass and revealed these facts to the prophets with such accuracy that we see their predictions being fulfilled as reported in the daily press.

VISIBLE KINGDOM ON EARTH 35

While men of skeptical and liberalistic tendencies are seeking to prove that the Bible is uninspired and have destroyed the faith of many and led them entirely away from the Word of God as of divine origin, our God, who knows the end from the beginning has met their false teachings with prophecies uttered thousands of years ago which are being fulfilled at the present time, giving us indisputable proof that "our rock is not as their rock, our enemies themselves being judges."

Moses utters a prophecy in Leviticus that is worthy of our notice. He is warning the people of the judgment that will come upon them if they depart from their divine covenant and trample upon the laws of God: "And I will destroy your high places, and cut down your images, and cast your carcases upon the carcases of your idols, and my soul shall abhor you. And I will make your cities waste, and bring your sanctuaries unto desolation, and I will not smell the savour of your sweet odors. And I will bring the land unto desolation: and your enemies which dwell therein shall be astonished at it. And I will scatter you among the heathen, and will draw out a sword after you: and your land shall be desolate, and your cities waste." Leviticus 26:30-33.

We will give one more quotation of prophecy concerning the dispersion of the Jews among their heathen neighbors. We read: "And the Lord saith, Because they have forsaken my law which I set before them, and have not obeyed my voice, neither walked therein; but have walked after the imagination of their own heart, and after Baalim, which their fathers taught them: therefore thus saith the Lord of hosts, the God of Israel; Behold, I will feed them, even this people, with wormwood, and give them water of gall to drink. I will scatter them also among the heathen, whom neither they nor their fathers have known: and I will

VISIBLE KINGDOM ON EARTH 37

send a sword after them, till I have consumed them." Jeremiah 9:13-16.

Unfortunate Jews! They have sinned grievously. They have been punished fearfully. They have suffered greatly. They not only broke their covenant with God, forsook His worship and went into the idolatry of their neighboring pagan peoples, but even those who had not gone so far as this rejected and secured the crucifixion of Jesus Christ. They mocked Him in His agony. When Pilate sought to release Jesus and declared Him innocent of any crime, and himself innocent of any desire to have Him crucified, they cried out, "Let his blood be on us and on our children." In other words, "If it is a sin to crucify this Christ we are willing to bear the responsibility of the sin. If there is any guilt, we invite the punishment for that guilt." Their prayer has been answered, and while through the centuries they have continued to reject Jesus they have suffered beyond human language to describe the agonies through which they have passed. The recent persecution of the Jews in Germany has driven a number of them to seek shelter in Palestine. The public press of October 28, 1933, gives an account of a new outbreak against these immigrant Jews by the Arabs. Some have been killed. Others have been wounded and they were only saved from a very general slaughter by the protection of British troops.

It is an interesting fact that the Hebrew people are indestructible. They have been a people without a country. They have wandered through the earth. They have been driven from one place to another. They have been robbed and taxed beyond all reason, and again and again they have been slain by thousands. But they have not and shall not be destroyed. They have preserved their identity. They are a separate and distinct people. They have mental capacity unsurpassed. Their business ability has

VISIBLE KINGDOM ON EARTH   39

made them masters of trade. In spite of all opposition they have forged to the front in all the fields in which they have labored, and in the midst of it all they have preserved the purity of their blood. A fine old Jew merchant said to me not long since, "Mr. Morrison, the Hebrew blood which flows in my veins is just as pure as the blood which flowed in the veins of King Solomon." He spoke with pride as he laid his hand with dignity upon his breast. The Scriptures very clearly teach that there is coming a better day for the Jews.

Any thoughtful person who is enough interested in the subject to examine the inspired records can but see that the prophecies concerning the scattering of the Jews among the nations of the earth and their oppression and sufferings, have been literally fulfilled.

CHAPTER IV.
THE RESTORATION OF THE JEWS.

There is a bright side to this whole Jew question. The prophets looking deep into the future discovered that, eventually, the times of chastisement would pass away and that the Lord would show mercy to His chosen people and restore them to the land of their fathers. I am quoting much Scripture in these pages in order to bring certain prophecies, with the truth they carry, before the reader. Many people read the Bible very little and a good many persons seem to read prophecy almost none at all, while some of those who do read prophecy give it some sort of a spiritual interpretation and fail to understand that the inspired seers are speaking of actual events which will take place among men here on our globe.

In our chapter on the dispersion of the Jews, we gave quite a lengthy warning from Moses on the captivity that would take place. That prophecy has been fulfilled. All the inspired predictions quoted in the chapter before this one have been fulfilled in a most remarkable way. We now give a prophecy spoken by Moses of the restoration of Israel and of their coming to be a spiritual people, obeying the laws of God and worshipping Him in spirit and in truth. We read: "And it shall come to pass, when all these things are come upon thee, the blessing and the curse, which I have set before thee, and thou shalt call them to mind among all the nations whither the Lord thy God hath driven thee, and shalt return unto the Lord thy God, and shalt obey his voice according to all that I command thee this day, thou and thy children, with all thine heart, and with all thy soul; that then the Lord thy God will turn thy captivity, and have compassion upon thee, and will return and gather thee from all the nations, whither the Lord thy God hath scattered thee. If

VISIBLE KINGDOM ON EARTH 43

any of thine be driven out unto the utmost parts of heaven, from thence will the Lord thy God gather thee, and from thence will he fetch thee: and the Lord thy God will bring thee into the land which thy fathers possessed, and thou shalt possess it; and he will do thee good, and multiply thee above thy fathers. And the Lord thy God will circumcise thine heart, and the heart of thy seed, to love the Lord thy God with all thine heart, and with all thy soul, that thou mayest live. And the Lord thy God will put all these curses upon thine enemies, and on them that hate thee, which persecuted thee." Deut. 30:1-7.

Isaiah was one of the greatest prophets. Much of what he spoke and wrote reads like a Gospel. He seemed to have seen and to have understood the coming Christ better than any one of the ancient seers. There is so much of Christ and of promise of mercy and blessing in Isaiah that we sometimes speak of this book as the "Gospel of Isaiah."

It is in his prophecy that we read: "Come now, let us reason together, saith the Lord: though your sins be as scarlet, they shall be as white as snow; though they be red like crimson, they shall be as wool." This is a wonderful Gospel promise. In the fifty-third chapter of Isaiah, we find one of the most remarkable foretellings of the crucifixion of our Lord. He describes His humble person, His silence before His accusers, the stripes which He received at His mock trial. He pictures Him as a man of sorrows and acquainted with grief. He speaks of Him as our Redeemer. "He was wounded for our transgressions, he was bruised for our iniquities: the chastisement of our peace was upon him." He calls attention to the fact that He suffered with the wicked and His grave was with the rich. It is an interesting fact that He was crucified between thieves and buried in a rich man's sepulchre. Then the veil of the future is lifted and the prophet declares with tri-

VISIBLE KINGDOM ON EARTH 45

umph, "He shall see of the travail of his soul and shall be satisfied."

Isaiah gives some most encouraging promises of the restoration of the Jews to the homeland of their fathers. We read: "For the Lord will have mercy on Jacob, and will yet choose Israel, and set them in their own land: and the strangers shall be joined with them, and they shall cleave to the house of Jacob. And the people shall take them, and bring them to their place: and the house of Israel shall possess them in the land of the Lord for servants and handmaids: and they shall take them captives, whose captives they were; and they shall rule over their oppressors. And it shall come to pass in the day that the Lord shall give thee rest from thy sorrow, and from thy fear, and from the hard bondage wherein thou wast made to serve." Isaiah 14:1-3.

Some years ago when I began to call attention to the prophecies concerning the restoration of the Jews to Palestine, a brilliant minister in his pulpit preachments for sometime majored on my ignorance of Palestine. He made it plain to his cultured audience, who were entirely indifferent to and totally ignorant of the prophecies contained in the Scriptures, that the Jews would not return to Palestine, first, because they were doing well where they were and did not want to return; second, the Turks owned Palestine and would not let the Jews return; third, there was no water in Palestine to enable the Jews or any one else to rebuild Jerusalem and develop the country; fourth, the land was so poor that it could not produce food for a population of any size; fifth, that the prophets did not mean what they said but were teaching spiritual truth which must be understood in order properly to interpret their meaning.

The trouble with this preacher was that he was more brilliant than wise. He trusted more to the ignorance of his audience than

VISIBLE KINGDOM ON EARTH 47

to the truthfulness of the Word of God. There is enough in the Bible about the Jews and Palestine that he did *not* know to make a very good-sized library of books. He was going to bring in the Millennium on the gallop without the coming of Christ. It was just around the corner.

First, he did not know that there was going to be a World War. Second, he did not know that Great Britain was going to drive the Turks out of Palestine and offer protection to the returning Jews. He did not know that the old aqueducts of Solomon would be cleaned out, repaired and bring abundance of water into Jerusalem. He did not know that the disintegrating limestone of Palestine would constantly renew the productiveness of the soil. He did not know that the greatest deposits of fertilizer in any one place on the globe lay waiting for "the time to come" in the bottom of the Dead Sea. He did not know that the Jordan would be harnessed to give light, heat, and power to Palestine. He did not know that there would arise in many countries a most bitter and aggressive persecution of the Jews which would lead them to seek peace in the homeland of their fathers. This brilliant minister knew so little of the whole matter of which he talked at random in ridicule and sarcasm that it would have been the part of wisdom for him to have kept quiet on the subject, but he was so full of brilliancy that there was no room left for wisdom. The dear man had not yet learned that when God speaks men should listen with attention and believe without doubt; when God makes a promise, however impossible it may appear, we may rest assured that He can work out the details and fulfill His promises. God has spoken with reference to the restoration of Israel. Hear Him:

"And I will sanctify my great name, which was profaned among the heathen, which ye have profaned in the midst of them; and the heathen shall know that I am the Lord, saith the Lord God, when I shall be sanctified in you before their eyes,

"For I will take you from among the heathen, and gather you out of all countries, and will bring you into your own land.

"Then will I sprinkle clean water upon you, and ye shall be clean: from all your filthiness, and from all your idols, will I cleanse you.

"A new heart also will I give you, and a new spirit will I put within you: and I will take away the stony heart out of your flesh, and I will give you an heart of flesh.

"And I will put my spirit within you, and cause you to walk in my statutes, and ye shall keep my judgments, and do them.

"And ye shall dwell in the land that I gave to your fathers; and ye shall be my people, and I will be your God.

"I will also save you from all your uncleannesses: and I will call for the corn, and will increase it, and lay no famine upon you.

"And I will multiply the fruit of the tree, and the increase of the field, that ye shall receive no more reproach of famine among the heathen.

"Then shall ye remember your own evil ways, and your doings that were not good, and shall lothe yourselves in your own sight for your iniquities and for your abominations.

"Not for your sakes do I this, saith the Lord God, be it known unto you: be ashamed and confounded for your own ways, O house of Israel.

"Thus saith the Lord God; In the day that I shall have cleansed you from all your iniquities I will also cause you to dwell in the cities, and the wastes shall be builded.

"And the desolate land shall be tilled, whereas it lay desolate in the sight of all that passed by.

"And they shall say, This land that was desolate is become like the garden of Eden;

VISIBLE KINGDOM ON EARTH 51

and the waste and desolate and ruined cities are become fenced, and are inhabited.

"Then the heathen that are left round about you shall know that I the Lord build the ruined places, and plant that that was desolate: I the Lord have spoken it, and I will do it.

"Thus saith the Lord God; I will yet for this be enquired of by the house of Israel, to do it for them; I will increase them with men like a flock.

"As the holy flock, as the flock of Jerusalem in her solemn feasts; so shall the waste cities be filled with flocks of men: and they shall know that I am the Lord." Ezek. 36:23-38.

This lengthy quotation from Ezekiel ought to be very convincing to those who believe the Bible and have any sort of interest in prophecy and especially in the present signs of the times. I wish to give our readers a prophecy by Jeremiah. It will be found in the thirty-second chapter, thirty-seventh to forty-fourth verses, and reads.

"Behold, I will gather them out of all countries, whither I have driven them in mine anger, and in my fury, and in great wrath; and I will bring them again unto this place, and I will cause them to dwell safely:

"And they shall be my people, and I will be their God.

"And I will give them one heart, and one way, that they may fear me for ever, for the good of them, and of their children after them:

"And I will make an everlasting covenant with them, that I will not turn away from them, to do them good; but I will put my fear in their hearts, that they shall not depart from me.

"Yea, I will rejoice over them to do them good, and I will plant them in this land assuredly with my whole heart and with my whole soul.

"For thus saith the Lord; Like as I have

VISIBLE KINGDOM ON EARTH 53

brought all this great evil upon this people, so will I bring upon them all the good that I have promised them.

"And fields shall be bought in this land, whereof ye say, It is desolate without man or beast; it is given into the hand of the Chal-de-ans.

"Men shall buy fields for money, and subscribe evidences, and seal them, and take witnesses in the land of Benjamin, and in the places about Jerusalem, and in the cities of Judah, and in the cities of the mountains, and in the cities of the valley, and in the cities of the south: for I will cause their captivity to return, saith the Lord."

We find in these prophecies the promise of a great spiritual awakening among the Jews returned to Palestine.

The fact that Jews in large numbers have returned and are now returning to Palestine, that land is being bought and titles given, new cities are springing up, and considerable industry manifesting itself, and valuable products being shipped out of Palestine into various countries, makes this prophecy of Jeremiah especially interesting. It seems that God, who knows the end from the beginning, has kept His promise that "when the enemy comes in like a flood He will lift up a standard against them." These prophecies are now being fulfilled and there is good reason to believe that in spite of opposition this great work will go forward and Israel will prosper. We have a prophecy by Ezekiel that this prosperity will arouse the cupidity of a northern power, called Gomer and Togarmah, which will move against Israel for war and robbery. We give the language of the prophet: "Thou shalt ascend and come like a storm, thou shalt be like a cloud to cover the land, thou, and all thy bands, and many people with thee. Thus saith the Lord God; It shall also come to pass, that at the same time shall things come into thy mind, and thou shalt think an evil thought: and thou

VISIBLE KINGDOM ON EARTH 55

shalt say, I will go up to the land of unwalled villages; I will go to them that are at rest, that dwell safely, all of them dwelling without walls, and having neither bars nor gates, To take a spoil, and to take a prey; to turn thine hand upon the desolate places that are now inhabited, and upon the people that are gathered out of the nations, which have gotten cattle and goods, that dwell in the midst of the land." Ezekiel 38:9-12.

It seems very clear here that this northern power, which is perhaps Russia, seeing that the Jews have been largely restored to Palestine and are prosperous and are developing great wealth from the bottom of the Dead Sea, will march with their armies against the returned Jews. The word is plainly written here: it will be some power out of the north. They, however, the prophet shows us, will meet with opposition. We read: "Sheba, and Dedan, and the merchants of Tarshish, with all the young lions thereof, shall say unto thee, Art thou come to take a spoil? hast thou gathered thy company to take a prey? to carry away silver and gold? to take away cattle and goods, to take a great spoil? Therefore, son of man, prophesy and say unto Gog, Thus saith the Lord God; In that day when my people of Israel dwell safely shalt thou not know it? And thou shalt come from thy place out of the north parts, thou, and many people with thee, all of them riding upon horses, a great company, and a mighty army: and thou shalt come up against my people Israel as a cloud to cover the land; it shall be in the latter days and I will bring thee against my land, that the heathen may know me, when I shall be sanctified in thee, O Gog, before their eyes."

We have quoted from the 13th to the close of the 16th verse of the 38th chapter of Ezekiel. This northern army we see will meet with opposition by "the merchants of Tarshish, with all the young lions thereof." That will probably be the forces of Great

VISIBLE KINGDOM ON EARTH 57

Britain. You know that Great Britain has a protectorate over Palestine. It is hardly probable that she would consent for any power to come up and destroy the returned Jews. If the reader will turn to the scripture from which we are quoting and read further he will find out that this conflict results in the destruction of the powers of Gog. You notice in the closing verse of this quotation this statement: "I shall be sanctified in thee, O Gog, before their eyes," that is, before the eyes of the heathen. In other words, if blasphemous Russia should take her mighty forces into Palestine to destroy the returned Jews and bring on war with Great Britain and should be destroyed it would be such a remarkable fulfillment of prophecy that people would be bound to admit the inspiration of the Bible and that the movement of events was in harmony with the teachings of the ancient seers of Israel. Let me suggest to the reader of this book that you read the thirty-eighth and thirty-ninth chapters of Ezekiel. It is not improbable that we have here a description of the final great conflict which is called the Battle of Armageddon.

We may be sure that some power will come from somewhere in the north to plunder returned Jews, and will be destroyed. I will close this chapter on the restoration of the Jews to Palestine with a quotation from each of the major prophets.

In Isaiah 65:17-22 we read:

"For, behold, I create new heavens and a new earth: and the former shall not be remembered, nor come into mind.

"But be ye glad and rejoice for ever in that which I create: for, behold, I create Jerusalem a rejoicing, and her people a joy.

"And I will rejoice in Jerusalem, and joy in my people: and the voice of weeping shall be no more heard in her, nor the voice of crying.

"There shall be no more thence an infant of days, nor an old man that hath not

VISIBLE KINGDOM ON EARTH

filled his days: for the child shall die an hundred years old but the sinner being an hundred years old shall be accursed.

"And they shall build houses, and inhabit them; and they shall plant vineyards, and eat the fruit of them.

"They shall not build, and another inhabit; they shall not plant, and another eat: for as the days of a tree are the days of my people, and mine elect shall long enjoy the work of their hands."

This glowing description of the future of the Hebrew people and the city of Jerusalem perhaps extends into the millennial age, and it very plainly reveals not only the physical, but the spiritual restoration of Israel. We now turn to Jeremiah 3rd chapter, 17, 18 verses. Also 16th chapter, 14 to 16.

"At that time they shall call Jerusalem the throne of the Lord; and all the nations shall be gathered unto it, to the name of the Lord, to Jerusalem: neither shall they walk any more after the imagination of their evil heart.

"In those days the house of Judah shall walk with the house of Israel, and they shall come together out of the land of the north to the land that I have given for an inheritance unto your fathers."

"Therefore, behold, the days come, saith the Lord, that it shall no more be said, The Lord liveth, that brought up the children of Israel, out of the land of Egypt;

"But, the Lord liveth, that brought up the children of Israel from the land of the north, and from all the lands whither he had driven them: and I will bring them again into their land that I gave unto their fathers.

"Behold, I will send for many fishers, saith the Lord, and they shall fish them; and after will I send for many hunters, and they shall hunt them from every mountain, and from every hill, and out of the holes of the rocks."

Take Jeremiah on the Restoration. We

VISIBLE KINGDOM ON EARTH 61

give that gracious prophecy found in the 23rd chapter, 2 to 8 verses.

"And I will gather the remnant of my flock out of all countries whither I have driven them, and will bring them again to their folds; and they shall be fruitful and increase.

"And I will set up shepherds over them which shall feed them: and they shall fear no more, nor be dismayed, neither shall they be lacking, saith the Lord.

"Behold, the days come, saith the Lord, that I will raise unto David a righteous Branch, and a King shall reign and prosper, and shall execute judgment and justice in the earth.

"In his days, Judah shall be saved, and Israel shall dwell safely: and this is his name whereby he shall be called, The Lord Our Righteousness.

"Therefore, behold, the days come, saith the Lord, that they shall no more say, The Lord liveth, which brought up the children of Israel out of the land of Egypt;

"But, The Lord liveth, which brought up and which led the seed of the house of Israel out of the north country, and from all countries whither I had driven them; and they shall dwell in their own land."

The prophet to some extent repeats himself. We now turn to Ezekiel. Take the 36th chapter of his prophecy 22 to 38 verses.

"Therefore say unto the house of Israel, Thus saith the Lord God; I do not this for your sakes, O house of Israel, but for mine holy name's sake, which ye have profaned among the heathen, whither ye went.

"And I will sanctify my great name, which was profaned among the heathen, which ye have profaned in the midst of them; and the heathen shall know that I am the Lord, saith the Lord God, when I shall be sanctified in you before their eyes.

"For I will take you from among the heathen, and gather you out of all countries,

VISIBLE KINGDOM ON EARTH

and will bring you into your own land.

'Then will I sprinkle clean water upon you, and ye shall be clean: from all your filthiness, and from all your idols, will I cleanse you.

"A new heart also will I give you, and a new spirit will I put within you: and I will take away the stony heart out of your flesh, and I will give you an heart of flesh.

"And I will put my spirit within you, and cause you to walk in my statutes, and ye shall keep my judgments, and do them.

"And ye shall dwell in the land that I gave to your fathers; and ye shall be my people, and I will be your God.

"I will also save you from all your uncleanness: and I will call for the corn, and will increase it, and lay no famine upon you.

"And I will multiply the fruit of the tree, and the increase of the field, that ye shall receive no more reproach of famine among the heathen.

"Then shall ye remember your own evil

ways, and your doings that were not good, and shall lothe yourselves in your own sight for your iniquities and for your abominations.

"Not for your sakes do I this, saith the Lord God, be it known unto you: be ashamed and confounded for your own ways, O house of Israel.

"Thus saith the Lord God; In the day that I shall have cleansed you from all your iniquities I will also cause you to dwell in the cities, and the wastes shall be builded.

"And the desolate land shall be tilled, whereas it lay desolate in the sight of all that passed by.

"And they shall say, This land that was desolate is become like the garden of Eden; and the waste and desolate and ruined cities are become fenced, and are inhabited.

"Then the heathen that are left round about you shall know that I the Lord build the ruined places, and plant that that was desolate: I the Lord have spoken it, and I

VISIBLE KINGDOM ON EARTH

will do it.

"Thus saith the Lord God; I will yet for this be enquired of by the house of Israel, to do it for them; I will increase them with men like a flock.

"As the holy flock, as the flock of Jerusalem in her solemn feasts; so shall the waste cities be filled with flocks of men: and they shall know that I am the Lord."

We see here a most remarkable promise not only of restoration to Palestine, but of a spiritual restoration, and it will be so remarkable and in such harmony with the Word of God, that it will compel belief in the existence of God, the inspiration of the prophets, and infallibility of the holy Scriptures. *"And they shall know that I am the Lord."*

There are so many gracious prophecies concerning the restoration and salvation of the Jews, that we would like to give the reader many pages yet but we close with Jeremiah 31:1-12.

"At the same time, saith the Lord, will I be the God of all the families of Israel, and they shall be my people.

"Thus saith the Lord, The people which were left of the sword found grace in the wilderness; even Israel, when I went to cause him to rest.

"The Lord hath appeared of old unto me, saying, Yea, I have loved thee with an everlasting love: therefore with lovingkindness have I drawn thee.

"Again I will build thee, and thou shalt be built, O virgin of Israel: thou shalt again be adorned with thy tabrets, and shalt go forth in the dances of them that make merry.

"Thou shalt yet plant vines upon the mountains of Samaria: the planters shall plant, and shall eat them as common things.

"For there shall be a day, that the watchmen upon the mount Ephraim shall cry, Arise ye, and let us go up to Zion unto the Lord our God.

VISIBLE KINGDOM ON EARTH 67

"For thus saith the Lord; Sing with gladness for Jacob, and shout among the chief of the nations: publish ye, praise ye, and say, O Lord, save thy people, the remnant of Israel.

"Behold, I will bring them from the north country, and gather them from the coasts of the earth, and with them the blind and the lame, the woman with child and her that travaileth with child together: a great company shall return thither.

"They shall come with weeping, and with supplications will I lead them: I will cause them to walk by the rivers of waters in a straight way, wherein they shall not stumble: for I am a father to Israel, and Ephraim is my firstborn.

"Hear the word of the Lord, O ye nations, and declare it in the isles afar off, and say, He that scattered Israel will gather him, and keep him, as a shepherd doth his flock.

"For the Lord hath redeemed Jacob, and ransomed him from the hand of him that was stronger than he.

"Therefore they shall come and sing in the height of Zion, and shall flow together to the goodness of the Lord, for wheat, and for wine, and for oil, and for the young of the flock and of the herd: and their soul shall be as a watered garden; and they shall not sorrow any more at all."

CHAPTER V.
WILL GOD SET UP A VISIBLE KINGDOM ON EARTH?

God's objective in the creation and redemption of man is far vaster than we can grasp, imagine, or understand. It reaches across the ages and out into eternity. We are assured, however, reading the Scriptures, that it embraces a divine order on this planet. Not only the redemption of individuals, but a period of righteousness and peace among men far beyond anything that has yet been attained. This fact is revealed as a part of His plan by the prophets, Christ, and the apostles.

The Bible with all it contains, Christ with all He taught and suffered, the Gospel with all it means and embraces, go to prove that it is God's purpose to bring divine order into His universe. In the angelic choir, which sang over the birth of Christ in Bethlehem, there is a prophecy of glory to God in the highest, peace and good will among men. The purpose of God is so great, His resources are so vast, His plan so perfect, and the spirit and teaching of the Scriptures are of a character which give us a blessed hope that some time in the future we are to have the Kingdom of God on earth, a kingdom of righteousness and peace.

The Lord Jesus taught His disciples and all who might become His disciples to pray, "Thy kingdom come, thy will be done on earth as it is in heaven." This prayer in itself embraces a prophecy and promise. It is unthinkable that Jesus would teach us to pray for something that is contrary to the will and plan of God or impossible of answer. No doubt this form of prayer is given us to keep in our mind the buoyant hope and glad thought that some day the powers of evil would be destroyed, wars would cease, and men would live in a world-wide brotherhood of confidence and co-operative fellowship.

VISIBLE KINGDOM ON EARTH 71

In his interpretation of Nebuchadnezzar's vision, Daniel tells us very positively: "In the days of these kings shall the God of heaven set up a kingdom, which shall never be destroyed: and the kingdom shall not be left to other people, but it shall break in pieces and consume all these kingdoms, and it shall stand for ever." Daniel 2:44. That Daniel's prophecies are quite worthy of belief is proven by the fact that much that he said in his interpretation of the king's dream has already become history. It will be remembered that he told Nebuchadnezzar, who had seen a great image with head of gold, breast and arms of silver, loins of brass, legs of iron, and feet partly iron and partly clay, that he, Nebuchadnezzar, was the head of gold, and that his rulership would be destroyed, that a kingdom represented by the breast and arms would take his place, that also would be overthrown and a third kingdom, represented by the loins of brass, would succeed it, and in time that kingdom would be destroyed by a power represented by the legs of iron, and eventually that would be broken up, divided into many small kingdoms with elements of disintegration and weakness mixed with elements of power like clay and iron.

This prophecy also has gone into history. Medo-Persia overthrew and destroyed the Babylonian Empire and took and held that vast region of country for a considerable period of time. No doubt in the prophecy of Daniel the Medo-Persian Empire was represented by the breast of silver. In due time, Alexander led the Grecian forces into this dominion and overthrew the Medo-Persian Empire and Greece for a time ruled that region. This was the loins of brass seen by Daniel. In course of time, Greece was conquered and succeeded by the Romans. They reached an acme of power in their iron rule never before equalled. They undoubtedly in the prophet's vision took the place of the legs of iron. By and by the

VISIBLE KINGDOM ON EARTH 73

power of Rome departed. She was rent asunder and her glory passed away and many kingdoms, represented by the feet and toes, took the place of Rome.

It is while these many powers are ruling that vast region with its many peoples that the kingdoms are to be broken up and God is to set up His kingdom, which "shall not be left to other people." It will not be under merely human government, but under divine rulership. Let it be remembered that Nebuchadnezzar in his vision saw "that a stone was cut out without hands that smote the image upon his feet that were of iron and clay, and brake them to pieces. Then was the iron, the clay, the brass, the silver, and the gold, broken to pieces together, and became like the chaff of the summer threshingfloors; and the wind carried them away, and no place was found for them: and the stone that smote the image became a great mountain and filled the whole earth." This stone we understand, is the Kingdom of God that shall break in pieces and sweep away all wicked and destructive human governments and bring in a reign of peace and righteousness.

The prophecies are full of gracious predictions of a reign of peace on earth. We call your attention to the proclamation by the prophet Micah: "But in the last days it shall came to pass, that the mountains of the house of the Lord shall be established in the top of the mountains, and it shall be exalted above the hills; and people shall flow unto it. And many nations shall come and say, Come, and let us go up to the mountain of the Lord, and to the house of the God of Jacob; and he will teach us of his ways, and we will walk in his paths: for the law shall go forth of Zion, and the word of the Lord from Jerusalem. And he shall judge among many people, and rebuke strong nations afar off; and they shall beat their swords into plowshares, and their spears into pruninghooks: nation shall not lift up a sword

VISIBLE KINGDOM ON EARTH 75

against nation, neither shall they learn war any more. But they shall sit every man under his vine and under his fig tree; and none shall make them afraid: for the mouth of the Lord of hosts hath spoken it." Micah 4:1-4.

It will be noticed here that wars shall cease, that nation shall not lift up the sword against nation. We are also pleased to see that the people are not to be crowded into cities, but they are to be agricultural. They will no doubt have small farms and live largely on vegetables, nuts, and fruits. They are to "sit every man under his vine and under his fig tree." They are not to be crowded together in unhealthy tenements. We note further, "and none shall make them afraid." The land-owner and the tax collector will not come around threatening to dispossess and cast them out. The earth will not be owned and dominated by a few people of vast wealth, but will be amicably divided up among the people and they will possess it in peace and plenty. As there will be no war or fear of war vast taxes will not be collected for the building of warships, great forts, and instruments of destruction. Men will not build forts along the borders of the nations, but vines and fig trees will grow along the borders and men will sit in peace and harmony eating the abundant fruit of moderate toil.

Isaiah gives a most beautiful prophecy of this time of peace among men and of the spirit of good fellowship and worship of God in spirit and in truth. We read: "The word that Isaiah the son of Amoz saw concerning Judah and Jerusalem. And it shall come to pass in the last days, that the mountain of the Lord's house shall be established in the top of the mountains, and shall be exalted above the hills; and all nations shall flow unto it. And many people shall go and say, Come ye, and let us go up to the mountain of the Lord, to the house of the God of Jacob; and he will teach us of his ways, and

VISIBLE KINGDOM ON EARTH 77

we will walk in his paths for out of Zion shall go forth the law, and the word of the Lord from Jerusalem. And he shall judge among the nations, and shall rebuke many people; and they shall beat their swords into plowshares, and their spears into pruninghooks: nation shall not lift up sword against nation, neither shall they learn war any more." Isaiah 2:1-4.

The similarity between the prophecies quoted here from Micah and Isaiah is striking, but not strange. They were both inspired men. They both spoke to the living certain great and gracious promises for the future and wrote for the generations to come. They saw the same great events and were in beautiful harmony with each other. Naturally so. Ministers of the Gospel who are true to the word of God are quite in harmony with each other in preaching the great fundamental doctrines of human sin, redemption in Christ, and salvation by faith. They often use the identical words, comparisons, and illustrations. There is nothing more interesting than the harmony of thought and expression among those who are redeemed of the Lord and enlightened and taught by the Holy Spirit.

Will God set up a visible kingdom on earth?

To doubt that God will in due time overthrow the tyrannical, selfish and unjust governments of the world and set up a kingdom of righteousness among men is to doubt the plainly written word of scripture. The failure of human governments, the confusion of the nations, the wars and rumors of wars with the vast preparations that are now going on among the most enlightened nations of the world, all become witness to man's failure and unfitness for the rulership of the world, and the necessity for the setting up of the kingdom of God on earth.

CHAPTER VI.
WHO WILL BE THE KING?

Having seen that it is the purpose of God to set up a Kingdom on the earth, the question naturally arises, Who will be the King?

We turn at once to the Scriptures for an answer to this question. Daniel has told us that this Kingdom which God shall set up after the destruction of all other kingdoms, shall not be left to the people. It is evidently, to have a Divine Ruler. See Daniel 7:13, 14, 27.

"I saw in the night visions, and, behold, one like the Son of man came with the clouds of heaven, and came to the Ancient of days, and they brought him near before him.

"And there was given him dominion, and glory, and a kingdom, that all people, nations, and languages, should serve him: his dominion is an everlasting dominion, which shall not pass away, and his kingdom that which shall not be destroyed.

"And the kingdom and dominion, and the greatness of the kingdom under the whole heaven, shall be given to the people of the saints of the most High, whose kingdom is an everlasting kingdom, and all dominions shall serve and obey him."

It is very evident from these verses that Christ is to be the King of this Kingdom which God is going to set up.

Turn to the first chapter of the gospel by Luke, and we have no difficulty in identifying our Lord Jesus Christ with the Divine Ruler of whom Daniel speaks. Read Luke 1:30-33 inclusive.

"And the angel said unto her, Fear not, Mary: for thou hast found favor with God.

"And, behold, thou shalt conceive in thy womb, and bring forth a son, and shalt call his name Jesus.

"He shall be great, and shall be called the Son of the Highest: and the Lord God shall give unto him the throne of his father **David:**

VISIBLE KINGDOM ON EARTH 81

"And he shall reign over the house of Jacob for ever; and of his kingdom there shall be no end."

This harmonizes with Micah 5:2:

"But thou, Bethlehem Ephratah, though thou be little among the thousands of Judah, yet out of thee shall he come forth unto me that is to be ruler in Israel; whose goings forth have been from of old, from everlasting."

Notice here he is to be "Ruler in Israel." He was born where the prophet Micah said he would be born. His time of rulership is sure to come. This is in harmony with Isaiah 9:6, 7.

"For unto us a child is born, unto us a son is given: and the government shall be upon his shoulder; and his name shall be called Wonderful, Counsellor, The mighty God, The everlasting Father, The Prince of Peace.

"Of the increase of his government and peace there shall be no end, upon the throne of David, and upon his kingdom, to order it, and to establish it with judgment and with justice from henceforth even for ever. The zeal of the Lord of hosts will perform this."

This is a glorious prophecy; it could not be more plainly written. This babe of Bethlehem is Jesus, the Christ, and this crucified, risen Christ shall sit upon the throne of David and inaugurate a government of justice and peace.

There are two very distinct groups of prophecies concerning Christ's coming into the world. One of these groups refers to the first coming of Christ in His humiliation, sufferings and atonement for the sins of the people; the other consists of predictions concerning the second coming of Christ in glory to reign over His redeemed people.

Here is where the Jews made their mistake, which proved so fatal to them. They did not "rightly divide the word of truth."

VISIBLE KINGDOM ON EARTH 83

They did not understand that in the restoration of the divine order in God's moral universe, it was necessary for Christ to come twice into the world, first as a sacrifice, second, as a King.

The Jews were looking for a king when they should have been looking for a Redeemer. They were not wanting a Christ to redeem them from sin; they wanted a ruler to break the Roman yoke and restore Israel to the glory of the reign of Solomon. They based their desires and expectations upon those splendid predictions and promises which will be fulfilled when Christ comes the second time, to rule.

No one can read and understand the prophecies, foretelling the Christ and his coming to live among men, with any sort of correct interpretation, who does not understand the two groups of prophecies, one with reference to His coming to suffer, the other with reference to His coming to reign.

Jesus admitted the fact in His trial, that

He was a King. It was not accidental, nor was it of human wisdom, that Pilate placed over the head of Christ at His crucifixion, "The King of the Jews." He was, He is, and He will be the crowned King of all kings.

Let us look at Isaiah 33:20-22:

"Look upon Zion, the city of our solemnities: thine eyes shall see Jerusalem a quiet habitation, a tabernacle that shall not be taken down: not one of the stakes thereof shall ever be removed, neither shall any of the cords thereof be broken.

"But there the glorious Lord will be unto us a place of broad rivers and streams; wherein shall go no galley with oars, neither shall gallant ship pass thereby.

"For the Lord is our judge, the Lord is our lawgiver, the Lord is our king; he will save us."

Here we have a glowing description of Christ's reign. Note verse 22: "The Lord is our judge, the Lord is our lawgiver, the

Lord is our King; he will save us." How clear, definite and positive are these promises.

What contrast this will be with the present world of dictators, in their tyranny, ignorance, pride and blasphemy.

We wish to give a quotation from Jeremiah, found in the 23rd chapter, 5th and 6th verses:

"Behold, the days come, saith the Lord, that I will raise unto David a righteous Branch, and a King shall reign and prosper, and shall execute judgment and justice in the earth.

"In his days Judah shall be saved, and Israel shall dwell safely: and this is his name whereby he shall be called, The Lord our Righteousness."

It appears to me that we shall be compelled to believe that the prophets foresaw the coming of Christ, and His reign as King, bringing righteousness and peace on earth, or we must conclude that the prophets did not know of what they wrote and spoke, thus rendering their predictions incapable of reasonable interpretation.

We must give you a quotation from Revelation 20:4, 5, 6.

"And I saw thrones, and they sat upon them, and judgment was given unto them: and I saw the souls of them that were beheaded for the witness of Jesus, and for the word of God, and which had not worshipped the beast, neither his image, neither had received his mark upon their foreheads, or in their hands; and they lived and reigned with Christ a thousand years.

"But the rest of the dead lived not again until the thousand years were finished. This is the first resurrection.

"Blessed and holy is he that hath part in the first resurrection: on such the second death hath no power, but they shall be priests of God and of Christ, and shall reign with him a thousand years."

If this is true, we can hold tenaciously to our blessed hope of the coming and reign of Christ; if it is not true, then to whom shall we go? Thank God, it is true, and while we wait with unshaken faith, we labor with zeal, that we may have some sheaves to offer our Christ at His coming.

I close this chapter with the words of our Lord Himself. "And Jesus said unto them, verily I say unto you, that ye which have followed me in the regeneration when the Son of man shall sit on the throne of his glory, ye also shall sit upon twelve thrones, judging the twelve tribes of Israel. Matt. 19:28.

Evidently our Lord is speaking here, not of what is to take place in heaven, but of what will take place on earth. The word of the Lord abideth forever.

CHAPTER VII.
JESUS CHRIST IS COMING BACK TO THIS EARTH.

That Jesus Christ is coming back to this earth in the visible body is so plainly taught in the Scriptures, we cannot understand how any one claiming to believe the Bible as the divinely inspired Word of God, and yet not believe in the Second Coming of Christ.

At His trial before the Jews, the high priest demanded of Christ to know if He claimed to be the Son of God. The answer of our Lord is found in Matthew 26:24: "Jesus saith unto him, Thou hast said: nevertheless I say unto you, Hereafter shall ye see the Son of man sitting in the right hand of power, and coming in the clouds of heaven."

At this saying of Jesus the high priest rent his clothes, thus expressing his height of indignation. Some of the high priests continue to rend, at least the air, when the coming of Christ is mentioned.

Turning to Acts 1:9, 10, 11, the following:

"And when he had spoken these things, while they beheld, he was taken up; and a cloud received him out of their sight.

"And while they looked stedfastly toward heaven as he went up, behold, two men stood by them in white apparel;

"Which, also said, Ye men of Galilee, why stand ye gazing up into heaven? this same Jesus, which is taken up from you into heaven, shall so come in like manner as ye have seen him go into heaven."

This is very clear testimony, and most reliable to those who accept the inspiration of the Scriptures.

King David was the great hymn writer for Israel. He was to the Jews what Charles Wesley was, and has been, to the Methodists. The book of Psalms was the

VISIBLE KINGDOM ON EARTH

hymn book of the Hebrew people. David was not only a poet, but also a prophet. He looked deep into the future, and saw and sang of Christ, both as Redeemer and King. Many of his psalms are descriptive of Christ's glorious coming to reign. Let us notice a few samples. In Psalm 96:13, we have: "For he cometh, for he cometh to judge the earth: he shall judge the world with righteousness, and the people with his truth." "When the Lord shall build up Zion, he shall appear in his glory." Psalm 102:16.

We could quote pages from David's songs descriptive of the coming and reign of Christ.

The final judgment will not take place at the second coming of Christ, but it will be a time of the overthrow of tyrannical and blasphemous governments, like that of Russia, the readjustment of the entire world program and rulership, and the punishment of many wicked people. For example, Hollywood will lose its place in the sun; the liquor oligarchy will go out of business; the godless congressmen, with Tammany and the lesser politicians, will go to their own place.

Isaiah speaks of the overthrow of the wicked at the coming of the Lord.

"And it shall be said in that day, Lo, this is our God; we have waited for him, and he will save us: this is the Lord; we have waited for him, we will be glad and rejoice in his salvation." Isa. 25:9.

"For, behold, the Lord cometh out of his place to punish the inhabitants of the earth for their iniquity: the earth also shall disclose her blood, and shall no more cover her slain." Isa. 26:21.

"Say to them that are of a fearful heart, Be strong, fear not: behold your God will come with vengeance, even God with a recompence; he will come and save you." Isa. 35:4.

"Behold, the Lord God will come with strong hand, and his arm shall rule for him: behold, his reward is with him, and his work before him." Isa. 40:10.

"For, behold, the Lord will come with fire, and with his chariots like a whirlwind, to render his anger with fury, and his rebuke with flames of fire." Isa. 66:15.

It would require too much space to give all that St. Paul said of the coming of the Lord, but we shall give a few quotations from his epistles which show how clearly he knew by inspiration that Christ would return to earth.

"For as often as ye eat this bread, and drink this cup, ye do shew the Lord's death till he come." 1 Cor. 11:26.

"Looking for that blessed hope, and the glorious appearing of the great God and our Savior Jesus Christ." Titus 2:13.

"To the end he may stablish your hearts unblameable in holiness before God, even our Father, at the coming of our Lord Jesus Christ with his saints." 1 Thess. 3:13.

"For they themselves shew of us what manner of entering in we had unto you, and how ye turned to God from idols to serve the living and true God;

"And to wait for his Son from heaven, whom he raised from the dead, even Jesus, which delivered us from the wrath to come." 1 Thess. 1:9, 10.

John the Beloved, gives his testimony to the coming of the Lord:

"And now, little children, abide in him; that, when he shall appear, we may have confidence, and not be ashamed before him at his coming." 1 John 2:28.

"Beloved, now are we the sons of God, and it doth not yet appear what we shall be: but we know that, when he shall appear, we shall be like him; for we shall see him as he is." 1 John 3:2.

We might continue to quote from the inspired writers, but what we have given should suffice for those who believe the

VISIBLE KINGDOM ON EARTH 95

Scriptures; those who do not so believe, are so thoroughly opposed to Christ and His coming that nothing will convince them, but Christ's glorious appearing in the heavens. Then they will be convinced:

"And the kings of the earth, and the great men, and the rich men, and the chief captains, and the mighty men, and every bondman, and every free man, hid themselves in the dens and in the rocks of the mountains;

"And said to the mountains and rocks, Fall on us, and hide us from the face of him that sitteth on the throne, and from the wrath of the Lamb:

"For the great day of his wrath is come; and who shall be able to stand?" Rev. 6:15-17.

What a tremendous shock the coming of the Lord will be to those who are opposed to His coming. How fearful to those who "have trodden under foot the Son of God, and hath counted the blood of the covenant, wherewith he was sanctified, an unholy thing, and hath done despite unto the Spirit of grace." Heb. 10:29.

What startling event the coming of the Lord will be to that army of preachers who deny His Virgin Birth and Godhead, and the blood atonement he made upon the cross, with all those vast multitudes who have followed after these false teachers. No doubt they will cry for the rocks to fall upon them, and the hills to cover them, "when the Lord Jesus shall be revealed from heaven with his mighty angels, in flaming fire taking vengeance on them that know not God, and that obey not the gospel of our Lord Jesus Christ; who shall be punished with everlasting destruction from the presence of the Lord, and from the glory of his power." 2 Thess. 1:7, 8, 9.

CHAPTER VIII.
WHAT SORT OF RULERSHIP WILL CHRIST GIVE THE WORLD?

Now that we have seen from the Scriptures that God will set up a visible kingdom on this globe, and that Christ will return to earth to be the King, we shall look into the Bible in order to ascertain what sort of government Christ will give to the nations of the earth.

First, the reign of Christ is to be supreme; it is to cover the entire earth. "It shall break in pieces and consume all these kingdoms."

"He shall have dominion also from sea to sea, and from the river unto the ends of the earth. They that dwell in the wilderness shall bow before him; and his enemies shall lick the dust. The kings of Tarshish and of the isles shall bring presents: the kings of Sheba and Seba shall offer gifts. Yea, all kings shall fall down before him: all nations shall serve him." Psalm 72:8-10.

Second, for the first time, the world of mankind will have a righteous government. "Behold, a king shall reign in righteousness, and a prince in judgment.' Isa. 31:1. Humanity has been burdened and crushed with tyrannical rulership. The history of the world is a history of human slavery, under the iron yoke of oppressive, heartless rulers, who have held their power, taxed and controlled the people by slaughter and bloody tyranny.

Isaiah gives us such a fine description of the rulership of Christ that we give it at some length:

"And there shall come forth a rod out of the stem of Jesse, and a Branch shall grow out of his roots:

"And the spirit of the Lord shall rest upon him, the spirit of wisdom and understanding, the spirit of counsel and might, the spirit of knowledge and of the fear of the Lord;

VISIBLE KINGDOM ON EARTH

"And shall make him of quick understanding in the fear of the Lord: and he shall not judge after the sight of his eyes, neither reprove after the hearing of his ears:

"But with righteousness shall he judge the poor, and reprove with equity for the meek of the earth: and he shall smite the earth with the rod of his mouth, and with the breath of his lips shall he slay the wicked.

"And righteousness shall be the girdle of his loins, and faithfulness the girdle of his reins.

"The wolf also shall dwell with the lamb, and the leopard shall lie down with the kid; and the calf and the young lion and the fatling together; and a little child shall lead them.

"And the cow and the bear shall feed; their young ones shall lie down together: and the lion shall eat straw like the ox.

"And the sucking child shall play on the hole of the asp, and the weaned child shall put his hand on the cockatrice' den.

"They shall not hurt nor destroy in all my holy mountain: for the earth shall be full of the knowledge of the Lord, as the waters cover the sea.

"And in that day there shall be a root of Jesse, which shall stand for an ensign of the people; to it shall the Gentiles seek: and his rest shall be glorious." Isa. 11:1-10.

Good old Mother Earth belongs to God and he will parcel it out to His children. "Blessed are the meek, for they shall inherit the earth."

Let Isaiah speak again of the glorious reign of Christ.

"In that day shall the branch of the Lord be beautiful and glorious, and the fruit of the earth shall be excellent and comely for them that are escaped of Israel.

"And it shall come to pass, that he that is left in Zion, and he that remaineth in Jerusalem, shall be called holy, even every one that is written among the living in Jerusalem:

"When the Lord shall have washed away the filth of the daughters of Zion, and shall have purged the blood of Jerusalem from the midst thereof by the spirit of judgment, and by the spirit of burning.

"And the Lord will create upon every dwelling place of mount Zion, and upon her assemblies, a cloud and smoke by day, and the shining of a flaming fire by night: for upon all the glory shall be a defence.

"And there shall be a tabernacle for a shadow in the daytime from the heat, and for a place of refuge, and for a covert from storm and from rain." Isa. 4:2-6.

We could continue to quote from the gracious promises of the reign of Christ on earth, and of the peace and happiness of mankind under his just rulership, but our space forbids. Read prophecy and believe what God has promised for the future and will fulfill. Your heart will be filled with praise and you will be strengthened for service.

The reign of Christ will be a reign of peace. "Men shall learn war no more." What a marvelous change that will be! A thousand years on this globe without war! Reader, let your mind run back over the past thousand years of human history; you will find it has been a thousand years of war, human slaughter, and all of the suffering and waste that accompany war, followed with its maimed, widows, orphans and heavy taxes in order to pay debts and pensions occasioned by war, and more extensive preparation for expected war.

The money spent by Europe, England and the United States in the World War, and still being spent because of it, would have built and endowed free hospitals for all of the sick, homes for all of the orphans, good houses for all of the poor, pensions for all of the old, provided for the education of

VISIBLE KINGDOM ON EARTH 103

all the youth of all the nations, drained all the swamps, built ample barriers to prevent the overflow of rivers, dams to hold the water sufficient for irrigation for all the plains, and furnished heat, light and power for all the people, free of charge.

The spirit of love and kindness, as we have seen from Isaiah, will bring peace and friendship between men and the animal kingdom. For the first time in human history the poor will have consideration, protection and an opportunity to enjoy life. Take Psalm 72:12, 13, 14 verses, "For he shall deliver the needy when he crieth; the poor also, and him that hath no helper. He shall spare the poor and needy, and shall save the souls of the needy. He shall redeem their soul from deceit and violence: and precious shall their blood be in his sight."

Under the gracious and just reign of Christ, the domination of corrupt politicians will pass away. The injustice and corruption of the courts will cease; the great trusts will be broken up, the entire liquor traffic, with its destruction of health and property, will be swept away. Many diseases that result from the violation of the laws of God and nature, will almost entirely disappear; people will not be crowded in unhealthy tenements in filthy streets of great cities.

CHAPTER IX.
WHEN WILL JESUS COME?

"For as often as ye eat this bread, and drink this cup, ye do shew the Lord's death till he come." 1 Cor. 11:26.

There is nothing in the whole realm of religion more solemn, more beautiful, more significant and more sacred than the sacrament of the Lord's Supper. In the institution of this Memorial the Lord Jesus purposed to keep us reminded of His death for us. The thought of that great redemptive act on the cross must be kept in mind. We are to remember that we were sinners, that Christ took our guilt upon Himself and died that we might be made free from our guilt, and by faith in Him, stand justified before God, and at peace with Him. These are major facts in the matter of our redemption that are not to be forgotten.

In partaking of this Memorial Sacrament, we should always recall the words of our Lord, "This cup is the New Testament in my blood which is shed for you." The atonement by our Lord was, and is, a blood atonement. It took His life to save us from the second death.

St. Paul teaches us that, when we bow in silent thought to receive the typical body and blood of Jesus, we are to look backward and forward; backward to the cross, with its innocent, suffering Victim, and forward with the blessed hope of His coming.

As millions of devout, trusting followers of Jesus have gathered at the sacramental altar through the centuries they have asked themselves, each other, and their religious teacher, "When will Jesus come?"

In times of severe religious persecution, and great suffering for the faith in, and witness for, Christ, the promise of His coming was far more dear to His followers, than in times when ecclesiasticisms were strong, with massive cathedrals, ornate forms of

VISIBLE KINGDOM ON EARTH 107

worship, palaces for residences of high office, and large salaries for ministering in soft speech to worldly and wealthy congregations. Why should such contented, comfortable people long for the coming of Christ? It is no evidence of great knowledge of the Scriptures, deep reverence, or devoted love for Christ, when men in places of power make the second coming of Christ a subject of jest. Were these jesters suffering persecution for Christ they might long for His appearing.

It is likely that fixing dates for the coming of the Lord has done more than any other one thing, discredited the promise of His return. In spite of the oft repeated teaching of Christ that the time of His coming is not, and will not be known to men, there is an eager class of devout people who will persist in fixing dates for His appearing. In times of sore distress men, in hope of His coming, are quite likely to get ahead of the divine program.

Our Lord anticipated this state of mind and eager longing of those who love Him, and gave this caution, when He said, "Ye shall hear of wars and rumors of wars: See that ye be not troubled; for all these things must come to pass, but the end is not yet. For nation shall rise against nation, and kingdom against kingdom: and there shall be famines, and pestilences, and earthquakes, in divers places. All these things are the beginning of sorrows. Then shall they deliver you up to be afflicted, and shall kill you: and ye shall be hated of all nations for my name's sake. And then shall many be offended, and shall betray one another, and shall hate one another. And many false prophets shall rise, and shall deceive many. And because iniquity shall abound, the love of many shall wax cold. But he that shall endure unto the end, the same shall be saved. And this gospel of the kingdom shall be preached in all the world for a witness unto all nations; and then shall the end come" Matt. 24:6-14.

VISIBLE KINGDOM ON EARTH 109

In this same chapter we find words from our Lord which are quite out of harmony with postmillennial teaching, that the entire human race will be brought into a state of salvation and righteousness before the coming of the Lord. We read: "For as the lightning cometh out of the east, and shineth even unto the west; so shall also the coming of the Son of man be. For wheresoever the carcase is, there will eagles be gathered together. Immediately after the tribulation of those days shall the sun be darkened, and the moon shall not give her light, and the stars shall fall from heaven, and the powers of the heavens shall be shaken; and then shall appear the sign of the Son of man in heaven: and then shall all the tribes of the earth mourn, and they shall see the Son of man coming in the clouds of heaven with power and great glory." Matt. 24:27-30.

We notice here that Christ shall come, not at the end of a thousand years of peace on earth, and righteousness among men, but at the close of a period of tribulation, perhaps during a period of tribulation. That the people, generally, will not be expecting Him at the time of His coming we find from the following: "But as the days of Noe were, so shall also the coming of the Son of man be. For as in the days that were before the flood they were eating and drinking, marrying and giving in marriage, until the day that Noe entered into the ark, and knew not until he flood came, and took them all away; so shall also the coming of the Son of man be." Matt. 24: 37-39.

Everything found in the New Testament on the subject of the second coming of our Lord goes to prove that that great event will come as a startling surprise to those who do not expect or desire His appearing. In his First Letter to the Thessalonians Paul says: "But of the times and the seasons, brethren, ye have no need that I write

VISIBLE KINGDOM ON EARTH 111

unto you. For yourselves know perfectly that the day of the Lord so cometh as a thief in the night. For when they shall say, Peace and safety; then sudden destruction cometh upon them, as travail upon a woman with child; and they shall not escape. But ye, brethren, are not in darkness, that that day should overtake you as a thief. Ye are the children of light, and the children of the day: we are not of the night, nor of darkness. Therefore, let us not sleep, as do others; but let us watch and be sober." 1 Thess. 5:1-6.

According to Christ, Paul and Peter, we find that the coming of Christ will be as great a surprise to the wicked, and as little thought of, as was the flood in the days of Noe; sudden as lightning, right in the midst of scoffing and ridicule of the whole subject. Peter says: "Knowing this first, that there shall come in the last days scoffers, walking after their own lusts, and saying, Where is the promise of his coming? for since the fathers fell asleep, all things continue as they were from the beginning of creation." 2 Pet. 3:3, 4.

It would be easy to collect many passages from Christ and the inspired writers showing that our Lord will appear in great glory.

In 1 Thess. 4:10, we read, "For the Lord himself shall descend from heaven with a shout, and with the voice of the archangel, and with the trump of God."

In Jude 1:14, we read, "And Enoch also, the seventh from Adam, prophesied of these, saying, Behold, the Lord cometh with ten thousand of his saints, to execute judgment upon all."

In Rev. 1:7, we read, "Behold he cometh with clouds, and every eye shall see him, and they also which pierced him; and all the kindreds of the earth shall wail because of him."

At His first coming, He came in humility to die for the sins of the people. He rode

VISIBLE KINGDOM ON EARTH

into Jerusalem on an ass's colt to die upon the cross for our redemption. He will come back in clouds of glory to sit upon the throne of universal empire and reign in righteousness and peace over His redeemed people.

How any one can accept the New Testament as a divinely-inspired volume and question, or deny these scriptures quoted here, we are quite unable to understand.

Our Lord Jesus gives us certain signs of His coming; events that will take place among men, that are as positive a proof of the nearness of His appearing as the swelling buds on the trees indicate that "summer is nigh at hand."

I cannot think it is irreverent, or an indication of ignorance or fanaticism, for the followers of Christ who are a bit tired of a war-torn world, reeking in drunkenness and sin of every kind, to long for the Lord to come and bring peace out of the strife, confusion and suffering that now ravage the earth.

Can it be inconsistent with intelligent Christian living, thinking and service, to study present human events and see if the swelling buds on the tree of prophecy give indications of the coming of our Lord? In the gospel record by St. Luke we find a prophecy of Jesus foretelling the destruction of Jerusalem, the slaughter and captivity of the Jews by the Romans, which has been fulfilled. It reads: "There shall be great distress in the land, and wrath upon this people. And they shall fall by the sword, and shall be led away captive into all nations: and Jerusalem shall be trodden down of the Gentiles, until the times of the Gentiles be fulfilled." Luke 21:23, 24.

This foretelling of Christ has been fulfilled in a most remarkable manner. So far as the destruction of the Holy City, and the captivity of the Jews are concerned, it looks now as if Jerusalem were coming back under Jewish domination. The saying of Christ, "Until the times of the Gentiles be

VISIBLE KINGDOM ON EARTH 115

fulfilled" indicates that Jerusalem shall not be permanently under Gentile control.

Reading further, Jesus says: "And there shall be signs in the sun, and in the moon, and in the stars; and upon the earth distress of nations, with perplexity; the sea and the waves roaring; men's hearts failing them for fear, and for looking after those things which are coming on the earth: for the powers of heaven shall be shaken." Luke 21:25, 26.

That we are living in a period of distress of nations will generally be admitted. There is perplexity, disagreement and contentions among statesmen, "whose hearts are failing them for fear." The National Conferences called to agree upon some plan to avert war, or at least, to postpone it, continue to fail to agree, meanwhile, all the nations are spending vast millions of money preparing for war. Magazine writers are constantly telling us of the fearful destruction of humanity the next war will bring.

The Lord does not tell us that out of the fearful conditions mentioned here, there will come peace among the nations, revival of business, restoration of confidence and great moral advancements, with widespread and far-reaching spiritual awakening, which will bring in a new era of progress and happiness among men. There is no such suggestion. At the close of these verses telling of the distress of nations, and men's hearts failing them for fear, we find Him saying, "And then shall they see the Son of man coming in a cloud with power and great glory." Luke 21:27.

Then Jesus goes forward with warning and exhortation to those who believe in and love Him, with these impressive words: "And take heed unto yourselves, lest at any time your hearts be overtaken with surfeiting, and drunkenness, and cares of this life, and so that day come upon you unawares. For as a snare shall it come upon all them that dwell on the face of the whole

VISIBLE KINGDOM ON EARTH 117

earth. Watch ye therefore, and pray always, that ye may be accounted worthy to escape all these things that shall come to pass, and to stand before the Son of man." Luke 21:34, 35, 36.

Following the teachings of our Lord on the subject of His return, and conditions that will exist on the earth directly before His coming, should we not, regardless of reproach and ridicule, see to it that we are robed in righteousness and our lamps trimmed and burning?

We shall let the Lord himself speak to our readers at the close of this chapter.

"Let your loins be girded about, and your lights burning;

"And ye yourselves like unto men that wait for their lord, when he will return from the wedding; that when he cometh and knocketh, they may open unto him.

"Blessed are those servants, whom the lord when he cometh shall find watching: verily I say unto you, that he shall gird himself, and make them to sit down to meat, and will come forth and serve them.

"And if he shall come in the second watch, or come in the third watch, and find them so, blessed are those servants.

"And this know, that if the good-man of the house had known what hour the thief would come, he would have watched, and not have suffered his house to be broken through.

"Be ye therefore ready also: for the Son of man cometh at an hour when ye think not."—Luke 12:35-40.

The remarkable fulfillment of those prophecies that promise the setting up of the Kingdom of God on earth, with Christ our King, with peace and good will among men, thrills millions of devout hearts with the hope that we are now nearing the end of a long and bloody age of war and human suffering, and the glorious appearing of our Lord Jesus Christ—"Even so, come, Lord Jesus."

CHAPTER X.
THE SIGNS OF THE COMING OF THE LORD.

Reading the Scriptures, we are led to believe that there are several great events that must take place before the Lord's visible coming. The first we mention is the preaching of the gospel to all nations.

Immediately before His ascension Jesus charged His disciples that they should tarry at Jerusalem until they were endued with power from on high; having received the Holy Ghost, they were to at once set forth to carry the gospel to the uttermost part of the earth. This is the tenor of Christ's teaching, everywhere, that the gospel of the redemption He had provided, must be given to all nations, with this conclusive statement: "And this gospel of the kingdom shall be preached in all the world for a witness unto all nations; and then shall the end come." Matt. 24:14.

Evidently, our Lord refers to the end of the Church Age, and the beginning of the Kingdom Age. Had the Church from the beginning kept in mind, ministry and faith the person, the baptism and offices of the Holy Spirit, no doubt, with the same enthusiasm of the early disciples, the gospel would have been preached to all nations long ago. The Christ who died to redeem the world, of course, desires the world to know of the death He suffered, the price He paid, and the redemption He wrought for the salvation of all mankind.

It is possible that if the Church had been faithful to this commission of our Lord the kingdom of righteousness and peace might have been set up on the earth long ago, and the carnage of war, drunkenness, sin and ruin which have been rampant in the earth the past five hundred years, might have been evaded. The Lord Jesus says nothing about the building of ecclesiasticisms to war with each other, the erection of vast cathe-

VISIBLE KINGDOM ON EARTH 121

drals at the expense of millions of dollars, the election of high officials to lord it over their brethren, dwelling in palaces, with salaries that tax and oppress the people; there is no hint of any such thing as this in the teaching of Jesus; in fact, the whole spirit of the New Testament is out of harmony with a very large per cent of what the Church has been engaged in. Jesus Christ did not die on the cross to establish vast ecclesiasticisms, but to set on foot an evangelism with burning heart and swift feet to carry His saving truth to all the inhabitants of the globe.

The failure of the Church to perform this task at the command, and in the spirit of her Lord, is a tragedy beyond words to describe, and the results have been fearful to contemplate. There are no words in the human language to depict the sorrow, suffering, human butchery and the loss of countless millions of souls, because of the failure of the Church to receive her baptism and hasten with the gospel to all men, everywhere.

It may be safely said, that the gospel has been preached in all nations, not as it should have been, but the movement and power of the gospel in the last few decades are most wonderful. It has become such a saving power that the modernists have become disturbed over the matter, and have sent out a group of elegantly garbed gentlemen, smelling strong of cigarettes, to "rethink missions," and put what stumblingblocks they may in the way of a rapidly spreading evangelism. It is remarkable what these "rethinkers" do not know about the powerful spiritual movements in India, China, Japan, Korea, Africa, in fact, all of the mission fields of the world. The gospel has been so generally preached among the nations of the earth, and is now going forward with such energy and holy enthusiasm, that we may safely believe we are rapidly nearing that period when this command of our Lord will have been fulfilled.

The second event we mention is the great apostasy. The Apostle Paul, in his second letter to the Thessalonians, cautions them against a too speedy expectation of the coming of the Lord, and tells them that before the appearing of Christ there will "come a falling away first, and that the man of sin be revealed, the son of perdition; who opposeth and exalteth himself above that is called God, or that is worshipped; so that he as God sitteth in the temple of God, showing himself that he is God."

I think it will be generally admitted that we are now in the midst of a great spiritual depression. The trend toward modernistic liberalism has become a powerful influence throughout the Christian Church. Destructive criticism had its origin, largely, in Germany; a half century ago it was having its blighting influence over the spiritual life of that great people. If a tree is to be judged by its fruit, the tree of destructive criticism was not good. It fruited in a World War of devastation and ruin.

The Hitler government has arrayed itself against evangelical religion. That part of the church which has allied itself with Hitler proposes to discard the Old Testament Scriptures, entirely; it even goes so far as to remove the cross from the churches in Germany, and the police have been breaking up Sunday schools. There is a startling spirit of persecution against Bible Christians, and a spirit of unbelief that amounts to blasphemy. The Church in Germany has reached a fearful state of apostasy.

Turning to Russia, there are no words to describe the spiritual dearth, the persecution of Christians, the rampant unbelief and blasphemy that spread like a black plague over Russia. Nothing like it has ever been known in the history of Christianity. The persecution has gone to the extreme, not only of the banishment of Christians to the frozen regions of Siberia, but to the merciless slaughter of helpless thousands of people. Russia's hatred of God, the transforming of cathedrals into halls for the promotion of atheism, her bloody persecution of Christians, her rapid preparation for war, and her violent attack upon the very foundations of Christian civilization place her apart, and separate, from all other nations, civilized or pagan. To recognize the Russian government and give her the right hand of fellowship appears to many, not only to be an insult to God, but to invite His coming judgments.

It is not worth while to try to hide from our faces the fact that modern liberalism is sapping the spiritual life of the English-speaking world which, heretofore, has been predominantly Protestant, evangelistic, and has largely furnished the missionary forces which have carried the gospel to pagan peoples. To deny that there has been a fearful departure from Bible truth, and belief in the Lord Jesus Christ, as pre-existent, and God manifest in the flesh, of virgin birth and making an atonement for sin on the cross, is to confess one's ignorance of present conditions, or positive proof that those who make such denials are doing so to cover up the fact while they propagate their unscriptural teachings.

The attack upon the virgin birth and blood atonement of our Lord Jesus has become so common among ministers of the various Protestant churches that it has almost ceased to provoke any serious comment or protest. The opposition to revivals of religion, even in Methodism, which was born in a revival, and once felt that her paramount mission was to assemble her people at least once a year in great spiritual campaigns and revival efforts, has become common and numbers of Methodist churches keep up their membership by taking in people who know nothing of repent-

VISIBLE KINGDOM ON EARTH 127

ance for sin, the regenerating power and witness of the Holy Spirit. Whether we are in the final apostasy that will characterize conditions immediately before the coming of our Lord or not, all thoughtful, devout people know that we are living in a period of sad decay of spiritual life, when false teaching, and the sowing of the seeds of doctrines entirely contrary to Bible Christianity, are broadcast among us everywhere.

The third event to which we call attention is that, as we approach the end of the age, perilous times will come. "Now the Spirit speaketh expressly, that in the latter times some shall depart from the faith, giving heed to seducing spirits, and doctrines of devils; speaking lies in hypocrisy; having their consciences seared with a hot iron." 1 Tim. 4:1, 2.

In his second letter to Timothy, Paul exhorts his son in the gospel with these words: "For the time will come when they will not endure sound doctrine; but after their own lusts shall they heap to themselves teachers, having itching ears; and they shall turn away their ears from the truth, and shall be turned unto fables. But watch thou in all things, endure afflictions, do the work of an evangelist, make full proof of thy ministry." 2 Tim. 4:3-5.

Referring to the third chapter of this same epistle, we have a remarkable description of present day conditions: "This know also, that in the last days perilous times shall come. For men shall be lovers of their own selves, covetous, boasters, proud, blasphemers, disobedient to parents, unthankful, unholy, without natural affection, false accusers, incontinent, fierce, despisers of those that are good, traitors, heady, highminded, lovers of pleasures more than lovers of God; having a form of godliness, but denying the power thereof: from such turn away." 2 Tim. 3:1-5.

Whatever any thoughtful person's attitude may be toward the second coming of Christ, we think all intelligent people who know anything about world conditions will admit that we are living in "perilous times." There has, perhaps, been no time in human history when there was less confidence in agreements between nations, when signatures of treaties were regarded as "scraps of paper," as at the present time. There has never been a time except periods when there was a floodtide of war and butchery, when the nations were so busy preparing for war against each other.

The description Paul gives in his letter to Timothy certainly applies to present conditions in our social, economic and domestic life. Greed has reached the limit. It was the greed of the millionaires of this nation openly avowed that provided the money, the false statement, and spirit that led to the repeal of the Eighteenth Amendment and turned the flood of liquor upon us. It was the bold, naked spirit of covetousness. The loss of natural affection is apparent in the prevention of birth, the love of dogs, children murdering parents and parents destroying their children, but the startling feature of it all is, that the apostle tells us that these people have a "form of godliness." They make profession of Christianity, are members of the church, and are utterly indifferent to the baptism, indwelling and leading of the Holy Spirit. The spirit of apostasy logically prepares the way and leads into the perilous times. When men cease to obey the laws of God they will cease to obey human laws; when they cease to love the Lord they will cease to love each other.

It occurs to us that, throughout the world, civilized and pagan, we are in the midst of perils; there are famines, earthquakes, floods, war, kidnapping, murders, suicides and personal liberty is disappearing from the earth. It appears that these four events in human history that are to take place as we approach the end of the age, are now taking place in all parts of the habitable world.

CHAPTER XI.

THE FAILURE OF HUMAN GOVERNMENTS.

In the early history of the human race men formed themselves into families which grew into tribes, which developed into nations. They soon found that, in order to any sort of successful development, there must be union of sympathy and action, and that they must have personal leadership. They chose their strongest and wisest men to lead their armies and direct and control their activities.

Thus, in due time, there were kings who, because of their courage in battle, and their wisdom in the administration and government of the people, came to be regarded as some sort of divine beings, and were given privileges in the matter of taxing the people, or seizing, at will, upon the property of individuals, marrying a multiplicity of wives, and taking, at their pleasure, beautiful women as their concubines, until they became human gods among their people who were superior to man-made laws.

As civilization advanced absolute monarchies, where the king or monarch had the life and death of all the subjects at the disposal of his own will were limited, parliaments came into existence and there was some limitation to the powers of crowned rulers. As years went by, people became more eager for larger freedom, despots were overthrown and more democratic forms of government were established among the more highly civilized nations.

With the setting up of the union of the States of this republic, and the writing of the Constitution which united these States, there was born the purest democracy that has ever existed among men. On this con-

VISIBLE KINGDOM ON EARTH 135

tinent men have lived with the safest protection and, at the same time, the largest liberty that has ever been enjoyed since men adopted forms of government for the controlling and directing the destinies of the people.

In this union of the States, for one hundred and fifty years, the individual has had opportunity and encouragement to develop himself to the limit of his inherent powers; meanwhile, he has been protected in life and property, and his rights, as a loyal and independent citizen, as nowhere else on this globe.

A hundred and fifty years is a comparatively short period of time in human history, and those of us who have lived the half of that period and noted, with interest and delight, the growth and development of this nation, have lived long enough to see a most remarkable change in the spirit and affairs of this republic.

For a number of years, the country has

largely been dominated and, many of its citizens of the poorer laboring classes enslaved, by a heartless Capitalism. The greed of wealth became so blind to the needs and rights of men that it has brought about a spirit of dissatisfaction and indignation which can easily go to a dangerous extreme of revolt, not only against Capitalism, but almost any sort of personal ownership of property, that will secure to the owner an income sufficient to permit said owner to live in comparative idleness and luxury.

In the last few months there has been such a radical change in the administration of governmental affairs that no one knows, with any degree of assurance today, what tomorrow may bring forth, and men are hearing, in a spirit of meekness and submission, voices of command and dictation that, a few decades ago, would have aroused the entire nation with a storm of protest that would have overthrown an administration.

VISIBLE KINGDOM ON EARTH 137

It is evident to all serious thinkers that the old order of individual thought, action and enterprise has passed away. It appears now that the Government will tell you what to plant, what to plow up; what to pay for having a suit of clothes cleaned and pressed; when you shall work and when you shall play. I am not entering a protest to the present regime, but simply calling attention to the radical change that has taken place, and to the fact that the wisest men do not know what to anticipate for the immediate or more distant future for this great nation.

Present conditions remind one of a letter that was written by Lord Macaulay, a member of the British Parliament, a noted historian and one of the great statesmen of his times, to Honorable H. E. Randall, of New York, in the year 1857. This letter appeared some time ago in the *Yale Review*.

We reproduce it for the thoughtful consideration of the readers of this volume.

"London, May 23, 1857.

"Dear Sir:

"You are surprised to learn that I have not a high opinion of Mr. Jefferson, and I am surprised at your surprise. I am certain that I never wrote a line, and that I never in parliament, in conversation, or even on the hustings—a place where it is the fashion to court the populace—uttered a word indicating the opinion that the supreme authority in a state ought to be intrusted to the majority of citizens told by the head; in other words, to the poorest and most ignorant part of society. I have long been convinced that institutions purely democratic must, sooner or later, destroy liberty or civilization, or both.

"In Europe, where the population is dense, the effect of such institutions would be almost instantaneous. What happened lately in France is an example. In 1848 a pure democracy was established there. During a short time there was a strong reason to expect a general spoilation, a national bankruptcy, a new partition of the soil, a maximum of prices, a ruinous load of taxation laid on the rich for the purpose of supporting the poor in idleness. Such a system would, in twenty years, have made France as poor and as barbarous as the France of the Carolingians. Happily the danger was averted; and now there is a despotism, a silent tribune, and enslaved press. Liberty is gone, but civilization has been saved. I have not the smallest doubt that if we had a purely democratic government here, the effect would be the same. Either the poor would plunder the rich, and civilization would perish, or order and property would be saved by a strong military government, and liberty would perish. You may think that your country enjoys an exemption from these evils.

"I will frankly own to you that I am of a very different opinion. Your fate I believe to be certain, though it is deferred by a physical cause. As long as you have a boundless extent of fertile and unoccupied land, your laboring population will be far more at ease than the laboring population of the Old World; and while this is the case, the Jeffersonian policy may continue to exist without causing any fatal calamity. But the time will come when New England will be as thickly peopled as Old England. Wages will be as low, and will fluctuate as much, with you as with us.

VISIBLE KINGDOM ON EARTH 139

"You will have your Manchesters and Birminghams. Hundreds and thousands of artisans will assuredly be sometimes out of work. Then your institutions will be fairly brought to the test. Distress everywhere makes the laborer mutinous and discontented, and inclines him to listen with eagerness to agitators who tell him that it is a monstrous iniquity that one man should have a million while another cannot get a full meal. In bad years there is plenty of grumbling, and sometimes a little rioting.

"But it matters little, for here the sufferers are not the rulers. The supreme power is in the hands of a class, numerous indeed, but select of an educated class, of a class which is, and knows itself to be deeply interested in the security of property and the maintenance of order. Accordingly, the malcontents are firmly yet gently restrained. The bad time is got over without robbing the wealthy to relieve the indigent. The springs of national prosperity soon begin to flow back again; work is plentiful; wages rise, and all is tranquillity and cheerfulness.

"I have seen England three or four times pass through such critical seasons as I have described. Through such seasons the United States will have to pass in the course of the next century, if not of this. How will you passs through them? I heartily wish you a good deliverance.

"But my reason and my wishes are at war, and I cannot help foreboding the worse. It is quite plain that your government will never be able to restrain a distressed and discontented majority. For with you the majority is the government, and has the rich, who are always a minority, absolutely at its mercy. The day will come when in the State of New York, a multitude of people, none of whom has had more than half a breakfast, or expects to have more than a half a dinner, will choose the legislature. Is it possible to doubt what sort of legislature will be chosen?

"On one side is a statesman preaching patience, respect for vested rights, strict observance of public faith. On the other is a demagogue ranting about the tyranny of capitalists and usurers, and asking why anybody should be permitted to drink champagne and to ride in a carriage, while thousands of honest people are in want of necessities. Which of the two candidates is likely to be preferred by a workingman who hears his children cry for bread? I seriously apprehend that you will, in some such season of diversity as I have described, do things which will prevent prosperity from returning; that you will act like people in a year of scarcity, devour all the seedcorn, and thus make the next year a year not of scarcity but of absolute distress. The distress will produce fresh spoilation. There is nothing to stay you. Your constitution is all sail and no anchor.

"As I said before, when society has entered on this downward progress either civilization or liberty must perish. Either some Caesar or Napoleon will seize the reins of government with a strong hand, or your Republic will be as fearfully plundered and laid waste by barbarians in the twentieth century as the Roman Empire was in the fifth; with this difference, that the Huns and Vandals who ravaged the Roman Empire came from without, and that your Huns and Vandals will have been engendered within your country by your own institutions.

"Thinking this, of course I cannot reckon Jefferson among the benefactors of mankind."

We are forced to admit that Lord Macaulay was able to look into the future and prognosticate with considerable accuracy the trend of present events in this country. What the end shall be, if there is an end, is unknown, and the wisest of men are living in a state of suspense and anxiety.

One thing is certain: Any sort of democratic government is disappearing from the earth. Russia is under the control of a blasphemous dictator who wields a power

VISIBLE KINGDOM ON EARTH 141

with a merciless despotism that surpasses that of any czar that was ever known in Russia. Turkey is under the dictatorship of Mustafa Kemal whose will is practically law. Riza Khan is dictator of Persia. Mussolini holds absolute sway of Italy. Adolph Hitler rules Germany with a rod of iron. Not only does he propose to dictate civil affairs, but he asserts his authority in the entire realm of the social and religious life of the people.

Thus, gradually, the wheels of progress for human freedom and individual initiative are turning backward and the world of mankind is being dominated with a spirit quite like that of the Dark Ages. There must be a deep and profound significance in these movements, so entirely out of harmony with the thought and spirit of a few decades ago. The strange thing about it all, is the fact that the spirit of freedom, which was asserting itself throughout the world, seems to have largely disappeared, and in the chaotic condition of the economic, social, political and moral world the people have become willing to surrender the higher things of the mind and soul, if they only secure food and clothing for their bodies.

The simple fact is, human rulerships through the centuries have proven failures. Man is a selfish being. He loves power and wealth, and when he secures power he seeks larger power and more wealth, regardless of the general welfare of those whom he governs. The history of the past, and conditions of the present are such that many people have been forced to the conclusion that we never shall have a rulership of equal justice, protection, of righteousness and peace among men, until Jesus Christ has been enthroned as King of kings and Lord of lords.

CHAPTER XII.
THE MAN OF SIN; OR, THE END OF THE AGE.

Reading the Scriptures it appears that God has broken up human history into ages, or periods of time, into which certain great events in the life of man on earth are to be developed and brought to a climax.

In the New Testament we sometimes find the expression, "The end of the world," when the more correct translation would have been, "the end of the age," or "an age." Great periods of time, or ages, come and go, but the world rolls on into millenniums of time.

There is a sense in which every age, or dispensation, of the gracious purposes of God goes forward preparing men for a larger revelation, a clearer conception of the divine Being, His will, His laws, His love for the human race and the developments of His plans for the redemption of mankind, and the bringing of perfect order into His moral universe.

There is not the slightest danger that the wheels of divine purpose will ever turn backward. God will never go into bankruptcy. His investments are so large, His resources are so vast, His time is so unlimited, His objectives are so glorious that He will move forward in the accomplishments of His plans until all intelligent beings shall acknowledge His infinite wisdom, the foes of Christ shall become His footstool, and "At the name of Jesus every knee should bow, of things in heaven, and things in earth, and things under the earth; and that every tongue should confess that Jesus Christ is Lord, to the glory of God the Father." Phil. 2:10, 11. And thus, the purposes of God are wrought, and His infinite plans go forward to the culmination of objectives so vast and glorious, that they are beyond human comprehension.

Prophecy clearly teaches that, as we approach the end of the present age, the judgments of God will be visited upon a rebel-

VISIBLE KINGDOM ON EARTH 145

lious people who have ruthlessly trampled His laws beneath their feet, rejected His mercy, mocked at and challenged His judgments. This is quite in harmony with past history. The Antediluvian age closed with the destruction of the wicked, who would not give heed to warning, repent of their sins and seek mercy. The righteous were selected and preserved while the wicked were swept away by the flood.

This was also true with the close of the Hebrew age. The Church had backslidden; the priests were false teachers; people had drifted into idolatry. The apostate Hebrew Church reached a climax in its rejection of their Messiah, the securing of His crucifixion, and the mocking and derision of Him in His agonies upon the cross. Having rejected mercy, there was nothing left for them but judgment. The true disciples of Christ fled to the mountains and were secure while Jerusalem was destroyed, and the Hebrew age went out in blood and fire.

The Hebrew age was a great improvement on the Antediluvian age. It gave us the prophets, the Old Testament Scriptures, and revelations of God as they had never come to men before, but it went out in apostasy and judgments, while the Church, or Christian age, came in as a new age, with one great mission to carry the gospel to every creature. That was to be the one great work of the Church age—to give the message of God's mercy and redemption in Christ to all nations, and thus to prepare the world of mankind for an age far superior to anything in the past.

The Lord Jesus never promised His disciples, or the Church which was to come out of their labors, an ideal state of things; it was to be a period of disagreement, of contentions, of strife, of persecution, of suffering, with imprisonments, and even death, of misconceptions of divine truth, of false prophets, of disasters, famines, earthquakes, pestilences, wars and rumors of

VISIBLE KINGDOM ON EARTH

wars. While the Church carried the gospel, in spite of all oppositions and persecutions, it was to keep praying "thy kingdom come; thy will be done on earth, as the angels do it in heaven."

This state of human society, described by our Lord during the Church age, would be the result of the selfishness and wickedness of mankind. The unfortunate outcome of disobedience to divine laws, and rejection of divine mercy, and in this way, producing the conditions that have existed throughout the nations during the Gospel age, and continue to exist today in the conflicts of nations, wars and bloodshed, all of which are contrary to the will of God, and the teachings of Christ. We are approaching the end of an age of sin, because sinful men have made it what it has been, and what it is.

The Scriptures teach that, as we approach the end of this age, there will appear a powerful personality, a genius for government, a military autocrat who will be endowed by the spirit of Satan himself. The inspired apostle calls this person "The Man of Sin," to whom we have referred in a previous chapter in this volume, where Paul tells us that he will "exalt himself above all that is called God, or that is worshipped; so that he as God sitteth in the temple of God, showing himself that he is God."

That such a being should appear, seemed impossible until recent trends toward bald atheism and blasphemy, such as had manifested itself in Russia, is manifesting itself in Germany, to say nothing of the organization of atheistic societies in this nation which seem to seek to exceed each other in blaspheming the God of the Bible, and exalting man as a being superior to Christ, as offered to us as a Saviour in divine revelation.

There is a reference to the Man of Sin as a great military leader at the head of the hosts gathered about him, invading Palestine, which invasion leads to the Battle of

VISIBLE KINGDOM ON EARTH 149

Armageddon. It reads: "Thus saith the Lord God; It shall also come to pass, that at the same time shall things come into thy mind, and thou shalt think an evil thought: (and margin has it, 'conceive a mischievous purpose') and thou shalt say, I will go up to the land of unwalled villages; I will go to them that are at rest, that dwell safely, all of them dwelling without walls, and having neither bars nor gates, to take a spoil, and to take a prey; to turn thine hand upon the desolate places that are now inhabited, and upon the people that are gathered out of the nations, which have gotten cattle and goods, that dwell in the midst of the land." Ezek. 38:10-12.

It is an interesting fact that the powers of those countries that have been persecuting the Jews seem determined, after having driven them out of their various countries, to follow them, even into Palestine, with their persecution and robbery. This evidently, will not take place until the returning Jews have become a considerable number and made remarkable progress in the accumulation of wealth.

We find in the prophecy of Daniel a number of references to the Man of Sin. In Dan. 8:23-25, we read: "And in the latter time of their kingdom, when the transgressors are come to the full, a king of fierce countenance, and understanding dark sentences, shall stand up. And his power shall be mighty, but not by his own power: and he shall destroy wonderfully, and shall prosper, and practice, and shall destroy the mighty and the holy people. And through his policy also he shall cause craft to prosper in his hand; and he shall magnify himself in his heart, and by peace shall destroy many: he shall also stand up against the Prince of princes; but he shall be broken without hand."

This prophecy of Daniel is in harmony with the teaching of the Apostle Paul in 2 Thess. 8:12. "And then shall that Wicked

VISIBLE KINGDOM ON EARTH 151

be revealed, whom the Lord shall consume with the spirit of his mouth, and shall destroy with the brightness of his coming: Even him, whose coming is after the working of Satan with all power and signs and lying wonders, and with all deceivableness of unrighteousness in them that perish; because they received not the love of the truth, that they might be saved. And for this cause God shall send them strong delusion, that they should believe a lie; that they all might be damned who believed not the truth, but had pleasure in unrighteousness."

Reading again from Daniel, with reference to this wonderful personality, we find the following: "And the king shall do according to his will; and he shall exalt himself, and magnify himself above every god, and shall speak marvelous things against the God of gods, and shall prosper till the indignation be accomplished: for that that is determined shall be done. Neither shall he regard the God of his fathers, nor the desire of women, nor regard any god: for he shall magnify himself above all. But in his estate shall he honour the God of forces: and a god whom his fathers knew not shall he honour with gold, and silver, and with precious stones, and pleasant things." Dan. 11:36-38.

John, in Revelation, gives quite a lengthy description of the tyranny and blasphemy of the Man of Sin. We read: "And there was given unto him a mouth speaking great things and blasphemies; and power was given unto him to continue forty and two months. And he opened his mouth in blasphemy against God, to blaspheme his name, and his tabernacle, and them that dwell in heaven. And it was given unto him to make war with the saints, and to overcome them: and power was given him over all kindreds, and tongues, and nations. And all that dwell upon the earth shall worship him, whose names are not written in the book of

VISIBLE KINGDOM ON EARTH 153

life of the Lamb slain from the foundation of the world." Rev. 13:5-8.

Reading farther, we find: "And he causeth all, both small and great, rich and poor, free and bond, to receive a mark in their right hand, or in their foreheads: and that no man might buy or sell, save he that has the mark, or the name of the beast, or the number of his name." Rev. 13:16, 17.

The Man of Sin, the false prophet and the beast are a sort of trinity associated with each other, heading up, from all the various dictators, which are prototypes of this final world dictator. The false prophet is the culmination of the diversity of false teachers of Eddyism, New Thought, New Theology, Modern Liberalism, and the conglomeration of false prophets and teachers, who are arraying themselves against the virgin birth, Godhead, redemptive power and glorious appearing of our Lord and Saviour Jesus Christ, who are destroying evangelical faith, leading the people away from the Word of God, grieving the Holy Ghost, and getting the masses ready to receive the mark of the beast, and worship the culmination of all evil in a mighty man who will dictate and control business operations so that, without the mark of the beast, no one can buy or sell, who will dictate the religious life of the people, persecute and slay the saints, as has been done in Russia, and as is being done in Germany, not yet, perhaps, up to bloodshed, and is being done in spirit and manipulation much more in the United States than most people are aware of.

It must be understood that the beast spoken of in Revelation is not a system, or an animal, but a person; one of this triumvirate supermen who, in their assumption of power, dictatorship and blasphemy, deceive the people and lead them to final judgment and destruction which is so clearly taught by Daniel and in the book of Revelation, when the vials of wrath shall be poured out

VISIBLE KINGDOM ON EARTH 155

upon the wicked. It must be remembered that finally, there is only one of two things that God can do with the individual sinner, or the rebellious nation, that is, pardon, or punish, and there is no possible way for Him to pardon those who will not repent, but continue in rejection of mercy and refusal to repent. Finally, there comes a time when the barren figtree must be cut down, whether it be a person, a nation, or the culmination of an age. We are told that "the beast and the false prophet are, and shall be tormented day and night, forever and ever," along with the Devil, who is to be cast with them into a lake of fire.

This inspired statement reveals the fact that the beast is a person, with individual responsibility, who is finally brought to judgment and punishment. We can scarcely imagine any king, emperor, or ruler more despotic, cruel, self-assertive and blasphemous than the steel dictator of Russia at the present time. Evidently, the world is far more ready to surrender itself to these three united personal forces, than most people suspect. Millions of people, everywhere, are ready at this very hour to receive that stamp, whatever it may be, that is called in scripture, "The mark of the beast."

People who are without God, with no spiritual light, no reverential fear, who are dominated by their selfish, carnal natures, who are under the influence of the lusts of the flesh, the pride of the eye, are ready to submit themselves to any dictator, however godless he may be, if they feel that would bring to them abundance of the things that minister to the body, regardless of the interests of their souls, which they have so far forgotten they possess, they feel no concern about them, either for this life, or that which is to come. Unbelief in the inspiration of the Scriptures, in the God of the Bible, in the redemptive work of Christ, in the personal presence of the Holy Spirit, is at high tide in Christian nations, and scarcely

VISIBLE KINGDOM ON EARTH 157

thought of among pagan peoples, and those countries which, for centuries, have been under the domination of Romanism.

In conclusion, we should like to offer a word of caution against a spirit of enthusiasm and unwisdom which hurries ahead of the divine plan and endeavors to bring in the Kingdom of God on earth before prophecy has been fulfilled, and the appointed time in the eternal mind. There should be no spirit of persecution, or railing on the part of those who look hopefully to the appearing of the Lord, against those who would delay the coming of the Bridegroom. The spirit of love and longing for Christ should be a spirit of patience, of love, of mission, of evangelism, of haste to gather in the harvest before the **breaking of the storm.**

The teachings of the prophets, Christ and the apostles with reference to His second coming have been damaged in the past by those who, in their eagerness, have gotten entirely ahead of the divine program. There must be caution here, but from the reading of the Scriptures, the disappearance of the spirit of democracy in the earth, the fearful apostasy from scriptural teaching, the rampant blasphemy and rejection of Christ, with the spirit of strife among the nations, the preparations for war, and the almost universal feeling among all classes of people, which has become a foreboding, that things cannot remain as they are, but that some tremendous and radical change is about to take place. May we not hope that we are approaching that golden age of which the prophets have spoken, statesmen have dreamed, and poets have sung, when God shall set up a visible kingdom upon earth, when Jesus Christ shall be crowned supreme Ruler over a world united in peace and harmony, and men shall learn war globe, wars shall cease, the spirit of broth- globe, wars shall cease, the spirit of brotherhood shall exist among all men, and "the earth shall be full of the knowledge of the Lord, as the waters cover the sea."

THE END

www.ingramcontent.com/pod-product-compliance
Lightning Source LLC
Chambersburg PA
CBHW031355040426
42444CB00005B/301